BRIGHT DARKNESS
JESUS——LOVER OF MANKIND

by

GEORGE A. MALONEY, S.J.

DIMENSION BOOKS
DENVILLE, NEW JERSEY

Imprimi Potest:
    Rev. Eamon Taylor, S.J.
    Provincial of New York Province
    January 1, 1977

    Published by Dimension Books, Inc.
    Denville, New Jersey 07834

-Dedication-

To Father Richard Lee, in gratitude for his friendship and cooperation as Dean of the John XXIII Institute for Eastern Christian Studies, without whom the Institute would not be what it is today.

ACKNOWLEDGEMENTS

Deepest gratitude to Sister Joseph Agnes of the Sisters of Charity of Halifax for reading and typing this manuscript, and for the kindness shown me by the Sisters of the Incarnate Word of Houston while I was writing parts of this book.

Copyright © 1977 by George A. Maloney, S.J.
All rights reserved

TABLE OF CONTENTS

INTRODUCTION		5
CHAPTER 1:	GOD PRESENT IN HIS WORD	9
CHAPTER 2:	JESUS, GOD'S SPOKEN WORD	27
CHAPTER 3:	JESUS CHRIST—EBED YAHWEH	47
CHAPTER 4:	THE KINGDOM OF GOD IS NEAR	68
CHAPTER 5:	GENTLE JESUS	88
CHAPTER 6:	JESUS HEALS	103
CHAPTER 7:	JESUS: HOLY, HOLY, HOLY	117
CHAPTER 8:	A NEW HEART	133
CHAPTER 9:	JESUS IN GLORY	153
CHAPTER 10:	JESUS SENDS HIS SPIRIT	171
CHAPTER 11:	JESUS PRESENT IN HIS BODY, THE CHURCH	186
FOOTNOTES		204

INTRODUCTION

We live our lives between noon and midnight, light and darkness, knowledge and ignorance, love and loneliness. There are moments when we seemingly move toward greater growth. There are also moments when we seemingly stop to rest, even to die a bit.

Simone Weil defined prayer as "a patient waiting with expectancy." And it is *prayer* that makes us human. The God-given potential within all of us cries out to be actualized by a self-surrendering act of love. All true love is prayer. In both there is the awful tension that combines absence and presence of the Beloved. In love of God and man there is the peaceful joy of the *already* mingled with the burning pangs of the *not yet*. In loving prayer there is always the returning to and the going away, the tender moments of possession and the agonizing search for the lost. It is in prayer that we become seekers who wish to look upon the face of God.

When Moses asked God that he might see Him, Yahweh answered:

> Here is a place beside me. You must stand on the rock, and when my glory passes by, I will put you in a cleft of the rock and shield you with my hand while I pass by. Then I will take my hand away and you shall see the back of me; but my face is not to be seen (Ex 33:18-23).

God is brilliant light and there is no darkness in Him (1 Jn 1:5). Yet as Yahweh spoke to Moses: "You cannot see my face for man cannot see me and live" (Ex 33:21). God has allowed us to see Him in His own Image, Jesus Christ (Col 1:15). Jesus is the Light of God refracted through the prism of the humanity He assumed from Mary, His Mother. In Him is the fullness of divinity (Col 2:9). In Him we see the presence of the Father (Jn 14:9).

Yet in that *brightness* of divinity that was allowed to shine forth in a moment of ecstatic transfiguration on Mt. Thabor, there was also *darkness*. Jesus Christ emptied Himself of His power and glory by taking upon Himself our humanity (Ph 2:7). He was like us in all things save sin (Heb 4:15). He entered into the darkness of man's sinful estrangement from God in the agony in the Garden. He screamed out in utter opaqueness to His Father's presence on the cross: "Eli, Eli, lama sabachthani—my God, my God, why have you forsaken me?" (Mt 27:46).

Jesus Christ, God-Man is *Bright Darkness.* He reveals to us the fullness of the Father and yet there is the darkness of faith that brings us to the light. We see God in Him, yet it is always darkly now, as in a mirror (1 Co 13:12). There is also the darkness of our sinful past that lurks as smoking clouds that surround the indwelling Light of God within our hearts. Even in deepest union in prayer with God, areas within us needing healing cry out for Christ to have mercy and bring us new life. We live in Him. He lives in us. And yet at the same time there is sin in our members (Rm 7:23-25).

A PRAYERFUL EXPERIENCE OF JESUS

Christian mystics down through the centuries have attempted to describe their inner experiences with God as "dazzling darkness," "brightness of most lucid darkness," "teeming desert." I have used the theme bright-darkness to present Jesus Christ to modern readers, hungry to meet Him in a prayerful experience. Jesus is divine and human, God and man, yet the prayerful experience of Jesus is an approach that brings together in paradoxical fashion, without separating, His dual natures.

The usual approach in writings that deal with Christology is either to emphasize the pre-existent Word, the Logos, of God who "comes down from Heaven" into our world and becomes man or to stress the human person, Jesus, whom the Father accepts on Calvary as His Divine Son. No one can ever present an adequate Christology that will express in human words the inexpressible Word of God. I do not want to disparage the work of speculative theologians in probing by use of human reason Revelation in order to articulate new knowledge about Christ.

But from the Christian East we can discover an approach that is a prayerful encounter with the mystery of God's transcendence in the area of experiencing the presence of Jesus as the loving communicating Word of God come into our world, dwelling within us in our "hearts" and revealing through His Holy Spirit "the breadth and the length, the height and the depth, until knowing the love of Christ, which is beyond all knowledge" (Ep 3:18) we are filled with the utter fullness of God.

Theology for the Greek Fathers is contemplative knowledge given by God to the humble of heart, to the broken and contrite, to the little ones of His Kingdom. Theology is an experience of entering into communication with the very life of God living within us. It is to participate in His inner life that can only be experienced in loving adoration.

JESUS GREW INTO INTEGRATION

In such a prayerful attitude towards Scripture one can be brought into a living encounter with Jesus. Jesus is the perfect human being but He grows into that perfection through His life situation. He strives through the catalyst of obedient love to His Father to surrender to the Holy Spirit in order to reach an integration of His unconscious with his consciousness, the feminine and the masculine, the dark potential of gentle receptivity and the aggressive light of conscious power of self-control.

To present the integrated person of Jesus in His *animus-anima* relationship, I have sought to present a theology of presence through God's Word. When God's Word becomes incarnate, God communicates His loving presence through Jesus as Suffering Servant, poor and humble, gentle and loving, compassionate and healing, dying and glorified, sending His Holy Spirit and being present in the living members of Jesus' Body, the Church.

My hope and prayer for all who read this book is from the words of St. Paul: "It is the same God that said, 'Let there be light shining out of darkness,' who has shone in our minds to radiate the light of the knowledge of God's glory, the glory on the face of Christ" (2 Co 4:6). May He bring the brightness of Christ into your darkness and make you light from Light!

George A. Maloney, S.J.
December 25th, 1976

CHAPTER 1

GOD PRESENT IN HIS WORD

The key question that Christians must ask themselves is not whether they believe that Jesus Christ is divine but whether they believe that God is Jesus-like. So many books and sermons, religion courses taught in schools and parishes have been concerned with proofs from the powerful deeds done by Jesus Christ that He truly is God. Such efforts can never change a human heart into a passionate lover of God.

The human heart has its own language of communication. It is love that speaks and makes the loved one *present* as a gift. Our hearts are hungry for God's love, for His gift of Self. And no syllogism or array of rational proofs will ever bring us to a similar, surrendering love.

When we adore a God of omnipotent power, we continually approach Him in the power of our intellect. But God speaks to us in His perfect Image (Col 1:15) that is Jesus Christ and God becomes present to us in His Word. But this Word is gentle, not overpowering. Only the meek and humble will open up to this Word and comprehend His message of love, which is the dynamic loving presence of the Trinity living within us.

LOVE IS PRESENCE

When we love another, we become a gifted presence to that person. We want to live in union with that person so as to be present as often as possible, not only physically in space and time but more importantly in the inner recesses of our consciousness. We become present to each other in deeper and deeper consciousness to the degree that we can share our most intimate thoughts through speech. Words are the most ordinary way of communicating our inner self as gift to the other. Without internal words that can be expressed in externalized words, spoken or written or acted out in gestures, we would never grow in love.

And we are this way as self-communicating beings because God is this way in His essence as Love. God the Father, in absolute silence, in a communication of love impossible for human beings to understand, speaks His one eternal Word through His Spirit of Love. In that one Word, the Father is perfectly present, totally self-giving to His Son. "In him lives the fullness of divinity" (Col 2:9).

But in His Spirit, the Father also hears His Word come back to Him in a perfect, eternal "yes" of total surrendering Love that is again the Holy Spirit. The Trinity is a reciprocal community of a movement of the Spirit of Love between Father and Son. Our weak minds cannot fathom the peace and joy, the ardent excitement and exuberant self-surrender that flow in a reposeful motion between Father and Son through the Holy Spirit. God becomes real only because He can communicate in Love with His Word. His Word gives Him His identity as Father. But that means eternal self-giving to the Other, His Word in Love.

GOD'S WORD IN CREATION

If God's essence is love, He seeks by His nature to share His being by communicating His presence. In the Judaeo-Christian religion, God becomes a God-toward-others by communicating Himself through His Word and His Spirit of love. God creates the whole world as good, as a sign of His burning desire to give Himself in faithful communication through His Word. The world at its interior is filled with the self-communicating Trinity. God is filling the universe with His loving Self. His uncreated energies swirl through and fill all creatures with His loving, creative presence.

> The word of Yahweh is integrity itself,
> all he does is done faithfully;
> he loves virtue and justice,
> Yahweh's love fills the earth.
> By the word of Yahweh the heavens were made,
> their whole array by the breath of his mouth.
> He collects the ocean waters as though in a wineskin,
> he stores the deeps in cellars.
> Let the whole world fear Yahweh,
> Let all who live in earth revere him!
> He spoke, and it was created;
> he commanded and there it stood (Ps 33:4-9).

God's creative Word, the Logos, is personified in the Old Testament as Wisdom itself. God delights to give Himself through His Word to His creatures.

> When he fixed the heavens firm, I was there,
> when he drew a ring on the surface of the deep,
> when he thickened the clouds above,
> when he fixed fast the springs of the deep,
> when he assigned the sea its boundaries
> — and the waters will not invade the shore —
> when he laid down the foundations of the earth,
> I was by his side, a master craftsman,

> delighting him day after day,
> ever at play in his presence,
> at play everywhere in his world,
> delighting to be with the sons of men (Pr 8:27-31).

Everything flows out of God's exuberant fullness of being and *becomes* a reality in His communicating Word. God is present in the heavens and on the earth. "Can anyone hide in a dark corner without my seeing him?—it is Yahweh who speaks. Do I not fill heaven and earth?—it is Yahweh who speaks" (Jr 23:24). And He speaks through His Word and oceans and mountains, birds and beasts, flowers and all living things spring into being under His laughing, joyful gaze. Nothing that is can escape His loving touch, His presence as Giver of life.

Not only does God communicate Himself in creation but He is a sustaining, directing God. He evolves His presence that is locked into His creation through His Word that is continually being communicated over millions of years.

GOD'S WORD SPOKEN IN MAN

Yet the millions of creatures do not image God's tremendous drive to communicate Himself more perfectly. From all eternity, God's Word spoken in all of creation was only as a means in order that this outpouring God could be present to one unique creation—man. The care and concern in this more perfect step of self-giving can be seen in the account of Genesis.

God is depicted as a self-communicating community, freely deciding on a new course of creative giving.

> God said, 'Let us make man in our own image, in the likeness of ourselves, and let them be masters of the fish of the sea, the birds of heaven, the cattle, all the wild beasts and all the reptiles that crawl upon the earth' (Gn 1:26).

Michaelangelo, in his famous Sistine Chapel painting of God's creation of man, pictures God as descending and touching man. God creates man, not as He does other things, already complete in their relationship of dependence upon God. A tree is a tree and cannot be anything else. God's imperative: "Let there be . . ." means that God's communication of Himself is fixed and determined to be given in only one way and in no other for a plant or an animal. But only man is *unfinished* and open-ended. In his first moment of existence, man is seen to be in communication with God. God speaks to him in the coolness of evening. Not only is man created by God as other creatures but he is created according to God's image and likeness.

His uniqueness, the early Greek Fathers saw, was not in being in the image of God, but, through possessing an intellect and will, man's uniqueness consists in being able to posit himself as an *I,* dependent on the Absolute *I* of God.[1] Jesus Christ, the Word made flesh, is the Image of God according to God's revelation in His Word-made-flesh.[2]

Emil Brunner captures the patristic understanding of man's relationship to the Image-Word of God in these words:

> God creates man in such a way that in this very creation man is summoned to receive the Word actively, that is, he is called to listen, to understand and to believe. God creates man's being in such a way that man knows that he is

> determined and conditioned by God, and in this fact is truly human. The being of man as an "I" is being from and in the Divine 'Thou,' or, more exactly, from and in the Divine Word, whose claim 'calls' man's being into existence. . . . The characteristic imprint of man, however, only develops on the basis of Divine determination as an answer to a call, by means of a decision. The necessity for decision, an obligation which he can never evade, is the distinguishing feature of man . . . it is the being created by God to stand 'over-against' Him who can reply to God, and who in this answer alone fulfills—or destroys—the purpose of God's creation.[3]

Man is, therefore, made according to God's Image—His Word. In the words of St. Irenaeus of the second century who summarizes well the whole patristic teaching on image and likeness: " 'for as the image of God did he make man' (Gn 9:6) and the *image* is the Son of God in whose image man was made."[4]

God would communicate Himself to man through His Word and He would progressively give Himself to man as He gives Himself to His own Word. God walks with man and dialogues with him in the cool of the day: a picture of peace and repose (Gn 2:8, 15). But before that familiarity could flower into a community of shared life, sin entered.

SIN—AN ABSENCE TO GOD

God's Word, spoken by God in man's heart and listened to by man in loving acceptance, was rejected by sin. Sin is an act whereby man closes his spiritual ears of conscience to God's Word. Man no longer wants to be present to God's loving presence. Although man can never stop God from being present in His gift of His spoken

Word, he can run from that presence and hide (Gn 3:10).

Man was meant to be open and docile to God's Word. His first step in realizing his potential as man in communication with God was to be like virgin earth. God's Word would fall gently upon its softness and take root. Yet man rejected being receptive and obedient, gentle and open. He wanted power to become like God (Gn 3:5) so he could rule his life in complete independence.

His sin was deafness to God's presence through His Word. In sinning, man also became absent (not present) to himself (Gn 3:17-19). Man, through sin, begins his long pilgrimage in exile, absent to the God who is ever present to him. God continually speaks His Word; but man is deaf. God is present, touching man in millions of ways, yet man is blinded to His presence.

Yet God is a consuming fire (Heb 12:29) and burns ardently to be present to man. He keeps the door open to man by promising him that He will establish a covenant. Through the offspring of the woman, He would crush the head of the serpent (Gn 3:15). Sin would be vanquished and man would gain ultimate victory in being restored to God's living and loving presence.

A COVENANT-PEOPLE

God chose one man, Abraham, to be the father of His People. Because he believed in God and obeyed Him faithfully, he was justified, for to such, God would again reveal His loving presence.

> I am El Shaddai. Bear yourself blameless in my presence, and I will make a covenant between myself and you, and increase your numbers greatly . . . Here now is my

covenant with you: you shall become the father of a multitude of nations. You shall no longer be called Abram; your name shall be Abraham, for I make you father of a multitude of nations. I will make you most fruitful. I will make you into nations, and your issue shall be kings. I will establish my covenant between myself and you, and your descendants after you, generation after generation a covenant in perpetuity, to be your God and the God of your descendants after you. I will give to you and to your descendants after you the land you are living in, the whole land of Canaan, to own in perpetuity, and I will be your God (Gn 17:2-8).

Through Isaac and Jacob and the twelve sons of Jacob, God began to fashion His new People. It was when the Egyptians began to oppress God's Chosen People that God revealed His Word in a new way. The encounter of Moses and Yahweh at the burning bush gives us insights to help us avoid objectivizing God's Word that He speaks to His People.

EHYEH ASER EHYEH

God is not a being who speaks a word, a thing. He is the absolute fullness of being who communicates Himself as a presence. Other beings are "unconcealed and gathered," in a word, are revealed in a process of becoming by God's loving involvement in the event wherein He speaks His Word.[5]

God speaks His Word from the burning bush that is not consumed. He shows that His Word is a revelation of His action. God is a concerned God and will reveal Himself progressively in His actions done for His Chosen People.

> And now the cry of the sons of Israel has come to me, and I have witnessed the way in which the Egyptians oppress them, so come, I send you to Pharaoh to bring the sons of Israel, my people, out of Egypt (Ex 3:9-10).

God's heart, imaged by the burning bush, is on fire with love for His People. God is touched by their sufferings. The Immutable bends down and suffers thirst, hunger, oppression along with His People.

Moses, like so many of us, wants to name God, "But if they ask me what his name is, what am I to tell them?" (Ex 3:13). And the Voice of God, His Word, comes thundering out of the burning bush: "Ehyeh Aser Ehyeh."

Much scholarly work has been done on this phrase that the translations from the Vulgate render as: "I am who am." Michael Allard brings together the work of many prominent biblical exegetes and explains the meaning of Ex 3:14. "Yahweh is not he who is, but he who will be, and even more particularly still, he who will be with."[6]

If we are to understand Jesus Christ as the living Word of God, not in static, objectivized terms of a hypostatic union of two *objects,* a divine and a human nature, but as an ongoing process of an involving God who reveals Himself in life's events, it is imperative that we grasp this important concept of God's revelation to Moses. This is to be God's only name whereby He will be known and adored by all generations. He is a God who will be with His people. But more importantly, He will become God, faithful, loving, protective presence among the oppressed, the poor, the broken and the humiliated. To those who need Him and cry out, He will condescend and become present as healing Love to them.

God is saying to Moses and to all of us that He cannot be confined in *one* word or name, much less, in one time or place. He is always forward and becoming God as Love in the needs of the next moment. If Moses wants to know or to experience God's true nature, he will find Him as a loving presence among the downtrodden. He is telling Moses that he will be present to God only by going down among His suffering people in Egypt and there he will encounter the true God.

God's actions in relieving sufferings from His children reveal His name: "I will be with you." God's Word is released as it "unconceals and gathers" His scattered children into a community, the *Qahal.* Moses will find God if he hears God's Word. But it is not a simple word that man can memorize; God's Word is heard when man goes down where God is, loving the poor and the oppressed.

When God's Word would reach full expression, as will be pointed out in later chapters, He would reveal again the same message that He gave to Moses: ". . . in so far as you did this to one of the least of these brothers of mine, you did it to me" (Mt 25:40).

GOD IN THE DESERT

As God lived out His promise to be a revealing presence of protective love among His People, He showed Himself present in the luminous cloud. No one could look upon God and live. But He longed to be with His People. He covers His *Shekinah,* His glory, by the cloud that hovers over the Israelites so He can be with them, day and night, guiding and protecting them (Ex 12: 21-22; 14: 19-20).

He was in the manna and quails that fed them, in the life-giving water that He gave them at Massah and

Meribah. He fought with them against the Amalekites and protected them against all opposing forces of nature. Yet God continues to reveal His presence as Word, becoming always more and more a concrete "place" where He would speak and the Israelites could enter into that place and communicate with Him.

As long as the Israelites journeyed in the desert, Yahweh promised to "pitch" His Tent among them. In that Tent, God spoke. His revealed Word to Moses on Mount Sinai—the ten Words—were engraved on stone and placed within the Tabernacle or Tent. But God's gathering Word was spoken anew from that place: "There I shall come to meet you; there from above the throne of mercy . . . " (Ex 25:22).

God's Word was in that Tent and anyone who wished to enter therein was promised a meeting with God.

> Moses used to take the Tent and pitch it outside the camp, at some distance from the camp. He called it the Tent of Meeting. Anyone who had to consult Yahweh would go out to the Tent of Meeting, outside the camp. Whenever Moses went out to the Tent, all the people would rise. . . . the pillar of cloud would come down and station itself at the entrance to the Tent, and Yahweh would speak with Moses. . . . Yahweh would speak with Moses face to face, as a man speaks with his friend (Ex 33:7-11).

But God spoke out of the context of being a God among His suffering people. His Word was an action. If God revealed His tender love for all the Israelites, He acted out this love in His Word. His Word is not separated from God who speaks the Word but He acts the spoken word out in the living context of His People.

Abraham J. Heschel has recalled this element in Judaism that Christianity has all too readily forgotten, that God is a searching, involving God.

> He is the father of all men, not only a judge; he is a lover engaged to his people, not only a king. God stands in a passionate relationship to man. His love or anger, his mercy or disappointment is an expression of his profound participation in the history of Israel and all men.[7]

Expressions of tender concern burst forth like meteors across the dark history of Israel's many infidelities, calling God's People back to His loving presence. "When you call to me, and come to plead with me, I will listen to you. When you seek me, you shall find me, when you seek me with all your heart" (Jr 29:12). God stoops down and picks up His child "like someone who lifts an infant close against his cheek" (Ho 11:4). He has carved His People "on the palms of my hands" (Is 49:16). And though a mother could ever forget her baby at the breast, "I will never you" (Is 49:15), implores Yahweh.

> I did forsake you for a brief moment,
> but with great love will I take you back.
> In excess of anger, for a moment
> I hid my face from you.
> But with everlasting love I have taken pity on you,
> says Yahweh, your redeemer (Is 54:7-8).

God is, therefore, indwelling the Tabernacle. But more really still is He in His little ones: the poor and humble, the widowed and orphaned. He who is awesome and absolute in His transcendence is one with the lowly in

His tender loving concern. He is a suffering God who truly suffers with His People as He also rejoices with their fortune, their acceptance of Himself as loving gift.[8]

Jurgen Moltmann, following the insights of Abraham Heschel, has well captured the understanding of God as suffering not only for and because of His People but also *with* them.

> Rabbis at the turn of ages spoke of a number of stages in the self-humiliation of God: in creation, in the call of Abraham, Isaac, Jacob and the history of Israel, in the exodus and in the exile. Ps 18:36: "When you humble me you make me great" was understood to mean, "You show me that you are great by your humiliation of yourself." God dwells in heaven and among those who are of a humble and contrite spirit. He is the God of gods and brings justice to widows and orphans. He is lofty, yet looks upon the lowly. So he is present in two opposite ways. God already renounces his honor in the beginning at creation. Like a servant, he bears Israel and its sins on his back. He descends into the thornbush, the ark of the covenant and the temple. He meets men in those who are in straits, in the lowly and the small. The accommodations of God to the limitations of human history at the same time contain the anticipations of the future indwelling in his whole creation, when in the end, all lands will be full of his glory. He enters not only into the situation of a limited creature but even into the situation of a guilty and suffering creature.[9]

If love is the presence of self-communicating oneself to the one loved—then God of the Old Testament is a humble, self-giving God through His spoken Word. We can so easily develop a theology of God, all perfect in Himself, and to Him we can attribute all powers and perfections. But it requires a broken and a contrite heart to accept a God who *needs* us! He pursues His People and suffers with them in order to break their pride and self-sufficiency. It is no wonder that God's involving Word, revealing and acting out God's humble condescension as He stoops to give Himself to man, would assume the personification of Wisdom itself.

THE WISDOM OF GOD

God spoke to His People through His chosen Prophets, especially Isaiah, Jeremiah and Ezechiel. These special friends of God became carriers of His Word, but only because they had received that Word into their own lives. They had experienced their own brokenness because they had experienced God's utter humility in pursuing them and their people. Like men of fire, they breathed forth their scalding denunciations against the stiff-necked Jews who were rejecting such a tender, loving God.

After the Exile the rebuilt Temple became not only the place of God's indwelling among His Chosen, but it became a sign of His universal love for all nations. God would free His People through the pagan prince, Cyrus, and thus He would utter His Word that would "unconceal and gather" all peoples into His Kingdom.

> Foreigners who have attached themselves to Yahweh to serve him and to love his name and be his servants—these I will bring to my holy mountain. I will make them joyful in my house of prayer. Their holocausts and their sacrifices will be accepted on my altar, for my house will be called a house of prayer for all the peoples. It is the Lord Yahweh who speaks, who gathers the outcasts of Israel: there are

others I will gather besides those already gathered (Is 56:6-8).

To gather all men into God's indwelling presence, God speaks His Word as Wisdom. God teaches men how they are to live humbly according to His Word. And so the Word now becomes the daughter of God and His helper in creating the universe (Pr 8:22-30; 3:19-20). She is always at His side, delighting Him day after day, ever at play in His presence, delighting everywhere in His World "to be with the sons of men" (Pr 8:30-31).

The Psalmist had personalized the Word or Speech of God as the creating Word. Psalm 33 clearly brings out God's creative presence through His Word. "Yahweh looks down from heaven and sees the whole human race. From where he sits, he watches all who live on the earth, he who moulds every heart and takes note of all men do" (Ps 33:13-15). Yet God desires through His Word to enter into a deeper, more intimate relationship with man. His Word as Wisdom conversed with and moved among men, Baruch tells us (Ba 3:37-38). Ben Sira teaches us

> They who eat me will hunger for more; they who drink me will thirst for more. Whoever listens to me will never have to blush. Whoever acts as I dictate will never sin (Si 24:21-22).

For Ben Sira, Wisdom, God's Word,.has been written down in the Sacred Books giving God's People the Law of Moses. Who keeps God's commands shows filial fear and love and will be blessed abundantly by God for reverencing His revealed Word.

God's Word is identified with this Wisdom in the Book of Consolation (Is 55:1-3, 6-11). It goes forth from the mouth of God to feed those who ardently hunger and thirst to receive it. His thoughts are different from men's; His ways are not ours.

God's Word as Wisdom is a spirit which loves men and educates them (W 1:5-6). She refuses to dwell in the hearts of perverse men (W 1:4) but she pours herself into pure hearts and makes them friends of God. She is the breath of the power of God, the splendor of His light, the image of His goodness. God loves only those with whom she dwells, those who love her, ask for her and receive her as a spouse (W 7:7-14; 22-28; 8:2). To such she assures incorruptibility and this brings man near to God (W 6:18-19). If man is guided and saved by her, he will live eternally with God in love (W 3:9; 5:15).

GOD PRESENT IN HIS TEMPLE

As God reveals His burning desire in His Word more clearly to be among His People, abiding and teaching, guiding and loving them in all events of their history, the Israelites correspondingly yearn to enter into His presence. The Temple in Jerusalem becomes the focal point in Jewish piety before the coming of the Word Incarnate. It is in the Temple that God dwells and communicates with men in a special manner. The House of God sanctifies Jerusalem and makes her impregnable to all enemies (Ps 46:5-6; 48:2-4, 9). Happiness consists in dwelling there.

> How I love your palace,
>   Yahweh Sabaoth!
> How my soul yearns and pines
>   for Yahweh's courts!
> My heart and my flesh sing for joy
>   to the living God.

> . . . Happy those who live in your house
>   and can praise you all day long;
> And happy the pilgrims inspired by you
>   with courage to make the Ascents!
>
> . . . A single day in your courts
>   is worth more than a thousand elsewhere;
> merely to stand on the steps of God's house
>   is better than living with the wicked (Ps 84:1-2, 4-5, 10).

To go into the Temple of Jerusalem and dwell there all the days of one's life, to gaze on Yahweh's holiness and loveliness in that blessed sanctuary becomes the cry not only of the Psalmist but of every believing Jew who could pilgrimage there on the great feasts. God's presence as communicating Word was felt powerfully in that holy dwelling place. All other presences of Yahweh among His People are summarized in this indwelling presence of God in the Temple. The yearning for God's presence is one that would create a temple, a dwelling place within man.

This dignity is still beyond man to imagine, that God would want not only to suffer with His People but also to dwell within each person. St. Paul grasped this ultimate climax of God's condescending love in communicating His Word to live within man when he wrote:

> Didn't you realize that you were God's temple and that the Spirit of God was living among you? If anybody should destroy the temple of God, God will destroy him, because the temple of God is sacred; and you are that temple (1 Co 3:16-17).

But the most the Jews could beg for was: "God, create a clean heart in me; put into me a new and constant spirit; do not banish me from your presence; do not deprive me of your holy spirit" (Ps 51:10). Like a few drops of rain falling on the mountain top, this desire for greater "presence" to God in His Word flows down the slopes and joins the other drops that form a cascading torrent that comes careening and crashing down the mountain to the ocean. God speaks in the hearts of men down through the many centuries before Christ's coming. Especially He speaks within the community of His People, the Anawim, the Remnant, that core of humanity who would be the carriers of this desire on the part of God to speak His Word and become present to mankind in such a way that that Word would never leave the human race. The Word of God would become flesh and in Him, Jesus Christ, God's presence, would be a living, speaking, suffering, loving Word in a human body, the true Temple of God. In that enfleshed Word of God, God would "unconceal and gather" together His universe and bring it into completion.

> Yes, God loved the world so much
> that he gave his only Son,
> so that everyone who believes in him may not be lost
> but may have eternal life.
> For God sent his Son into the world
> not to condemn the world
> but so that through him the world might be saved (Jn 3:16-17).

CHAPTER 2

JESUS, GOD'S SPOKEN WORD

Herman Hesse, in his novel, *Journey to the East*, describes a group of pilgrims on a mythical journey. Leo is the central figure who is a loving, serving presence to the others in the group. He does all the lowliest chores, buoys up their spirits by his laughter and song. As long as Leo is with them, all goes well. But then Leo suddenly disappears and the group falls apart, abandoning the journey.

The narrator of the story, after several years of traveling, comes upon Leo and is brought to the monastery of the Order that sponsored the journey. Inside he discovers that Leo was the Superior of the Order. He had been the Superior all the time on that journey but his real leadership was in his humble role as servant. By the quality of his inner being, shown in his presence toward each person on the journey, Leo called others into being. His presence was an activating force towards others.

God is ever present as a serving Word spoken in our history at all times. God can never be without His communicating Word for God is love and love is presence in loving service to the other. For Christians the central point in human history, the point toward which all other events in preceding human history were to reach fulfilled meaning and from which all future events would unfold in integrated meaningfulness, was the Incarnation.

> The Word was made flesh,
> he lived among us,
> and we saw his glory,
> the glory that is his as the only Son of the Father,
> full of grace and truth (Jn 1:14).

God has spoken definitively His Word in the person, Jesus Christ. Everything that God has spoken in His actively creating Word is fulfilled in Him.

> At various times in the past and in various different ways, God spoke to our ancestors through the prophets; but in our own time, the last days, he has spoken to us through his Son, the Son that he has appointed to inherit everything and through whom he made everything there is. He is the radiant light of God's glory and the perfect copy of his nature, sustaining the universe by his powerful command; and now that he has destroyed the defilement of sin, he has gone to take his place in heaven at the right hand of divine Majesty. So he is now as far above the angels as the title which he has inherited is higher than their own name (Heb 1:1-4).

APPROACHES TO THE WORD MADE FLESH

From the New Testament we discover various ways of approaching God's Word in Jesus Christ. In some texts the writers begin with the human Jesus who lived and died as any other human being but "God has made this Jesus whom you crucified both Lord and Christ" (Ac 2:36). This Jesus "was proclaimed Son of God in all his power through his resurrection from the dead" (Rm 1:4).

Other texts emphasize God's unique salvific presence in and through Jesus Christ. "... God in Christ was reconciling the world to himself . . . " (2 Co 5:19). " . . . we were reconciled to God by the death of his Son . . . " (Rm 5:10). God gives us salvation through what Jesus Christ has done, especially by becoming the fully active Word of God in His sufferings and death.

Still other scriptural texts show the Son of God as enjoying a pre-existence. Like Hermes in mythology, God's eternal Word enters into humanity by taking upon Himself flesh. "In the beginning was the Word: the Word was with God and the Word was God. He was with God in the beginning" (Jn 1:1-2). Such texts, especially in the Johannine and Pauline writings, highlight God's great love in sending His Son (Jn 3:16), who was equal with God, but emptied Himself for our sakes (Ph 2:6-8).

Many texts combine Christ's divinity and humanity by highlighting His role as an image of the Heavenly Father. In such texts Jesus, both in His divinity and in His humanity, mirrors the Father for us. For St. Paul, Jesus Christ " . . . is the image of the unseen God and the first-born of all creation . . . " (Col 1:15). Jesus confesses to the disciple Philip: "To have seen me is to have seen the Father . . . " (Jn 14:9). Jesus is the only way to the Father because He alone knows the Father and therefore has the power to reveal Him to all who accept His testimony.

And finally, other texts place Jesus Christ in a cosmic setting. Not only have all things been created in Him (Jn 1:3; Col 1:16), but He is Lord of the Universe, inside of human evolutive history directing all things to their fullness. He is the Recapitulator. God " . . . would bring everything together under Christ, as head, everything in the heavens and everything on earth" (Ep 1:10). Jesus Christ is the Alpha and the Omega (Rv 1:8). He is the First and the Last, the Living One (Rv 1:17). God ". . . has put all things under his feet, and made him, as the ruler of everything, the head of the Church, which is his body, the fullness of him who fills the whole creation" (Ep 1:23).

This has led W. Pannenberg to speak of christologies characterized as "from above" and "from below."[1] R. H. Fuller analyzes the sources of such christological approaches. Among the Hellenistic converts to Christianity there developed the hypostasizing of the pre-existing Logos that came down from Heaven to take on flesh.[2]

St. Justin Martyr and other second century Apologists, along with St. Irenaeus, Tertullian and Origen, developed this approach. The Alexandrian School, so heavily influenced by Philo and Middle Platonism, reached its peak of expression in the "Logos-flesh" christology of Sts. Athanasius and Cyril of Alexandria.

The "from below" christology centered its origin in the Palestinian Jewish Christian Church (Jesus Christ "adopted" a Son of God at the second coming) and in the Hellenistic Jewish groups of the Diaspora ("adoption" at the Ascension and Jesus' present lordship).[3] The Antiochene School that opposed the Alexandrian theologians and was defeated in the Councils of Ephesus (431) and Chalcedon (451) was headed by such thinkers as Paul of Samosata, Theodore of Mopsuestia and Nestorius. Today many leading Catholic and Protestant theologians, inspired by Schleiermacher, such as Bultmann, Gogarten, Tillich, Pannenberg, Rahner and Schoonenberg, stress the human development of Jesus as He "becomes" the Son of God.

AN APOPHATIC CHRISTOLOGY

Who can ever present an adequate christology that will express in human words the inexpressible Word of God?

Jesus Christ is a beautiful diamond, shining brilliantly in our darkness and reflecting rays from His Heavenly Source, the Father. Man takes one position and sees truth in one ray. Jesus is God from all eternity. But another ray flashes across the first, not negating, but showing a new beauty of the eternal Diamond. He is also a total human being.

Man needs to articulate and define certain doctrines about the objective Jesus Christ. We are not free to make up our own ideas about God's only begotten Son who became man for us. God has spoken His Word in the Incarnation. The Gospel does give us the historical Jesus, believed in by the first Christian community. The Church gives us the skeleton but tells us there is more to the living Jesus Christ that escapes the ordinary way of human thinking. The Resurrection is in the *kerygma* or preaching of the Church, but the kerygma is in the Eucharist, which is the living memorial of the Resurrection and its most immediate experience.[4] St. Irenaeus in the second century had described it: "Our doctrine is in the Eucharist and the Eucharist confirms it."[5]

AN EXPERIENTIAL CHRISTOLOGY

For the Eastern Churches, with their apophatic stress on the mystery of God's transcendence, theology is essentially an "experience." St. Maximus wrote: "Experience is knowledge itself in action which comes from beyond all thought."[6] Such contemplative knowledge, by participation that God gives to the humble of heart, is true *theology,* called by the Greek Fathers *theognosis.* Theology is to enter into communication with the life of God. It is to participate in His inner life that can only be experienced in loving adoration. To become a theologian, as Evagrius of the 4th century said, is to pray and if one prays, one will be a theologian.[7]

To write about theology means to agree to live this revealed Truth and, if one must at all costs speak, to try to relate the content, so inexpressible, in a way that objectivization will not exclude mystery or the living communication between God and man. God is not above; He is to be found ahead, as we anticipate His willingness to communicate Himself to us through His Living Word. To do "christology" is to participate in the living reality of the Christ who by the Spirit offers Himself to us every day in the private communion of prayer, in the offering of the Eucharist, in the Word of the Bible, in the assembly of Christians and in each man encountered and given to us by God to serve and heal by His loving power within us.

I do not wish to disparage the work of theologians down through the ages of Christianity. I merely wish to point out the impossibility of any one "rational" presentation of Jesus Christ to give an adequate appreciation of the mystery that He is and always will be for us. Each approach has some merit and highlights some facet of the great depths of beauty in Jesus Christ. But who of us "with all the saints, has strength to grasp the breadth and the length, the height and the depth, (Ep 3:19) of the love of Jesus Christ, which is beyond all knowledge? Who of us can ever be filled with the utter fullness of God?

Because God in Jesus Christ is in relationship to us, depending on our starting point, theologians will always describe a descending or an ascending christology. But I would like to present Jesus Christ from a different approach. It is another ray reflected from Him, the Light of the world. Perhaps this more contemplative aspect can offset the either/or, *from above* or *from below* christologies that no longer speak to our contemporary world.

GOD PRESENT IN HIS WORD

To understand how Jesus Christ is God's definitive, communicating presence to us and yet that He is always a dynamic revelation of God's love for us in each moment, let us examine the Hebraic meaning attached to Logos.[8]

In the first epistle of St. John we see the Word of God, Jesus Christ, described in terms of the original Hebraic understanding of *dabar.*

> Something which has existed since the beginning,
> that we have heard,
> and we have seen with our own eyes;
> that we have watched
> and touched with our hands:
> the Word, who is life —
> that is our subject (1 Jn 1:1).

Philo and the Stoics, writing in Greek, hypostasized *Word* into an independent principle of rationality and order. In the Old Testament, and surely also in the mind of the writer of the Johannine corpus, *Word* (*Dabar,* in Hebrew) is a dynamic concept, totally dependent on God who communicates His Word to man. Otto Procksch gives a linguistic analysis of *Dabar* in the Old Testament.[9] *Word* in the Hebraic sense has a *dianoetic* content. *Word* in Scripture presents the reader with a thought whereby a thing is known through a concept. The inner nature of a thing is revealed, "unconcealed," made manifest by means of the *word.*

Another element in *Dabar* is the dynamic power that the *word* releases in the receiver of the word. The *word* is charged with creative power and energy that flow from the *word* into the receiver, transforming him somewhat into the *word* and the *mind* speaking the word.

Both of these aspects are found in God's Word in the Old Testament. Precisely because God progressively is communicating Himself as a God among His oppressed people, always faithful in His futuristic involvement in power to bring them into fullness of life, His Word in the New Testament assumes more concretely these aspects of revealing His nature through His Word made flesh and releasing His power into the receiver of His Word.

ST. JOHN'S WORD

When the Johannine Prologue uses *Logos,* according to G. Kittel,[10] there is no stress placed on an abstract objectivization or personification of the Logos. The evangelist desires to trace the origin of the glory beheld in Jesus Christ. And that origin is the eternal creative activity of God's Word. The reader is easily brought back through the parallelism used to the same creative activity of God's Word in the Genesis account of creation.

Both accounts begin with the phrase "In the beginning," which takes us back to the same moment of creation. In Gn 1:1-4, there is a contrast between emptiness and solitude, with darkness covering everything and the light that God "saw was good." Then ". . . God divided light from darkness." In Jn 1:3-4, there appears a similar contrast of "nothingness" as opposed to "life," since all things are created through the Word of God, which Word was the ". . . life (that) was the light of men, a light that shines in the dark, a light that darkness could not overpower" (Jn 1:4-5).

From the very first word of his Prologue, John wishes to establish the Word's role, not only in human salvation but also in the entire cosmos. He uses pre-existing language to contrast that God's Word is always unchangeably united with God in contrast to the changing, becoming, material, finite world. God's Word stands outside of anything finite. It is a free gift that God will give beyond man's control. R. Bultmann puts it:

> Rather, the mythological terminology is intended to express the absolute and decisive significance of his word—the mythological notion of pre-existence is made to serve the idea of Revelation. His word does not arise from the sphere of human observation and thought, but comes from beyond. It is a word free of all human motivation, a word determined from outside himself . . . Therefore his word is not subject to men's scrutiny or control. It is an authoritative word which confronts the hearer with a life-and-death decision.[11]

Many scholars quoted by Kittel have pointed out that John wanted to contrast the living aspect of the Word in Jesus Christ in opposition to the Torah that at the time of Christ had become personalized. The Torah was conceived as pre-existing in God. Now John gives to Christ all of these prerogatives of the Torah. "In him the eternal word of God, the word of creation, the word of the law, is not just passed on, but enacted. Christ is not just a teacher and transmitter of the Torah. He is himself the Torah, the new Torah."[12]

The Torah Word was extrinsic to the mind of God. John's choice of the word *Logos* is made to show precisely God's dynamic relationship with the created world through the creative function of His Word. He wishes to tell us that the Word's function is to reveal the nature of God that is independent of the created world, even though the Word will be revealed in history as the Light moves into the Darkness.

John establishes immediately a breathtaking perspective that covers the whole universe that ever was, is or ever will be. It is in the presence of the perfect possessor of all being that we watch the created world slowly begin to move under the dynamic power of God's Word from the coldness of nothingness into the warmth of being. It is the Word that brings the universe from its existence in the mind of God into actual existence. It is not a static role that began and is now finished. Wherever created beings are coming into existence or moving to a greater degree of existence, there the Logos is operative. For there can be no progression in being except through the Logos who is the source of all being.

GOD'S GLORY IN JESUS

Throughout the Old Testament, God's presence as communicating power, coming down to dwell and protect His people gradually became externalized as His indwelling glory," His *shekinah*. John is telling us that that progressive dwelling of God in His powerful glory is now fully realized in Jesus Christ. ". . . and we saw his glory, the glory that is his as the only Son of the Father, full of grace and truth" (Jn 1:14).

In describing the Incarnation, John uses a Greek word that puns on the Hebrew word *shekinah*. God's Word "pitches His tent" (Greek verb: *skenoun*). In this word we see the *s-k-n* of *shekinah,* but *this* Word is the *glory* of God now dwelling among us human beings.

Perhaps John was thinking of the beautiful passage from the Book of Ecclesiasticus:

> I had my tent in the heights
>   and my throne in a pillar of cloud.
> ... Over the waves of the sea and over the whole earth,
>   and over every people and nation I have held sway.
> Among all these I searched for rest,
>   and looked to see in whose territory I might pitch camp.
> Then the Creator of all things instructed me,
>   and he who created me fixed a place for my tent.
> He said, "Pitch your tent in Jacob,
>   make Israel your inheritance."
> From eternity, in the beginning, he created me,
>   and for eternity I shall remain (Si 24:4-9).

God stayed among His chosen people in the tabernacle of the Lord. Now God speaks His loving Word and "pitches His tent or tabernacle" and dwells among the newly chosen people of Israel. This active Word of God, that was, from the beginning, creating new relationships with His people, now centers His presence in the "tent" of human flesh. John identifies the Word that created the universe and rules it by His power with the man of flesh that began to exist and whom John personally had seen and touched, Jesus Christ.

> ... and we saw his glory,
> the glory that is his as the only Son of the Father,
> full of grace and truth (Jn 1:14).

The glory of God's divinity shone through the frailness and lowliness of His humanity. The glory or power of God in His Word radiated in the teachings and miracles of this man Jesus. God's grace and life flowed through this man. He touched people, looked upon them, loved them, spoke to them. His humanity is the point of encounter as once in the desert the tabernacle was through which the life of God could flow into the lives of all who accepted Him. His sublime teachings were the *brightness* of God's own truth that turned men from the *darkness* of the ungodly and the sinful into children born, not of flesh but "of God himself" (Jn 1:13).

Jesus Christ is the New Law, the Torah. For as the Israelites received God's life and truth through the Jewish Law given them by Moses, now life and truth have become incarnate in the person of Jesus Christ.

> Indeed, from his fullness we have, all of us, received—
> yes, grace in return for grace,
> since, though the Law was given through Moses,
> grace and truth have come through Jesus Christ.
> No one has ever seen God;
> it is the only Son, who is nearest to the Father's heart,
> who has made him known (Jn 1:16-18).

St. Paul plays on a similar theme of the indwelling presence of God's glory now made visible in Jesus.

> Both Jew and pagan sinned and forfeited God's glory and both are justified through the free gift of his grace by being redeemed in Christ Jesus who was appointed by God to sacrifice his life so as to win reconciliation through faith (Rm 3:23-25).

The literal translation of v. 25 is: "whom God put forward as a propitiatory through faith by his blood." The *propitiatory* or throne of mercy, spoken of in Ex 25:17 and

Heb 9:5 was the golden lid which covered the Ark of the Covenant in the desert and in the Temple. It symbolized Yahweh's throne where He was present and working on behalf of His people. Paul, like John, is saying that God is now present in this Word-made-flesh, Jesus Christ, in His liberating power.

The Epistle to the Hebrews describes this Word-Man, Jesus Christ, in similar terms of glory and power: "He is the radiant light of God's glory and the perfect copy of his nature, sustaining the universe by his powerful command" (Heb 1:3).

The glory of Jesus Christ is an imaging of the glory of the Father and has nothing of its own. His glory is a self-giving love in dependence on the Father. "If I were to seek my own glory that would be no glory at all; my glory is conferred by the Father, by the one of whom you say, 'He is our God' although you do not know him. But I know him. . . . and I faithfully keep his word" (Jn 8:54-55).

Jesus Christ, therefore, is the Word of faith in the sense that He perfectly and faithfully represents His Father in human communication of words and actions. Everything He says or does is *the* Word of God. God no longer needs to speak through Prophets (Heb 1:1-2). Jesus speaks God's complete presence to His people. Whether He touches a leper and heals him or claims absolute authority to forgive sins, Jesus is God communicating His Word. His actions, as Bultmann says, are a speaking; whatever He says is action.[13]

JESUS CHRIST—LIGHT

Light in the Bible is used in several ways. It can refer in a general way to living a good moral life (e.g. Jn 3:20). Or, as often in the Old Testament, it can refer to an extrinsic code, like the Law of Moses. But more often in the New Testament, Jesus Christ is the Light that brings healing salvation to those who sit in darkness or in the death of sin. Jesus is God present to His people and bringing them eternal life.

> I am the light of the world;
> anyone who follows me will not be walking in the dark;
> he will have the light of life (Jn 8:12).

Jesus Christ, God's presence made flesh, has come into the world as a light, so that no one who believes in Him might remain in darkness (Jn 12:46). Darkness in the New Testament usually refers to the world that is absent to God's presence. In such a world there is not God's life, but only death.

Jesus came as the fulfillment of Isaiah's prophecy.

> The people that walked in darkness
> have seen a great light;
> on those who live in a land of deep shadow
> a light has shone . . .
> they rejoice in your presence.
> . . . For there is a child born for us,
> a son given to us
> and dominion is laid on his shoulders;
> and this is the name they give him:
> Wonder-Counsellor, Mighty God,
> Eternal Father, Prince of Peace (Is 9:1-6).

He was the Light yet the darkness strove to extinguish the Light. God had sent Him as His saving presence, a loving presence among isolated and lonely people, starved for love and yet "men have shown they prefer darkness to the light because their deeds were evil" (Jn 3:19). Those who receive Jesus as God's Light into their hearts accept and live by the truth of Jesus' Spirit. Such come out into the light by doing all in God (Jn 3:21).

We accept Jesus as Light and we live in Him and He lives in us. We know this experientially when Jesus gives us His Spirit who brings us into union with one another.

> But if we live our lives in the light,
> as he is in the light,
> we are in union with one another
> and the blood of Jesus, his Son,
> purifies us from all sin. . . .
> Anyone who claims to be in the light
> but hates his brother
> is still in the dark.
> But anyone who loves his brother is living in the light
> and need not be afraid of stumbling . . . (1 Jn 1:7; 2:9-10).

Jesus is a Light that demands a choice: either we choose to let Him become God's presence in us, in our words and actions to the world of men through His loving Spirit loving in us all men or we crawl back into our dark isolation of self-love and thus reject life-giving love. In the words of the poet, W.H. Auden: "We must love one another or die."

JESUS CHRIST—LIFE

Jesus' words bring salvific light to man's intellect. But they are not static truths but life-giving. He is Light that removes the darkness of sin but His Light also causes Life. They who accept Jesus as God's Light, to live by His commands, will have the Light of Life (Jn 8:12).

Jesus is the fullness of God's Life and He alone can give it to us. "I have come so that they may have life and have it to the full" (Jn 10:10). True, eternal life has been given by the Father to Jesus.

> . . . through the power over all mankind
> that you have given him,
> let him give eternal life to all those you have entrusted to him.
> And eternal life is this:
> to know you,
> the only true God,
> and Jesus Christ whom you have sent (Jn 17:2-3).

Knowing God is to enter into a whole way of life. It is being caught up into a liberating, tender love on the part of the omnipotent God, made manifest as a spoken Word in His Son, Jesus Christ. "We can be sure that we know God only by keeping his commandments. . . . But when anyone does obey what he has said, God's love comes to perfection in him. We can be sure that we are in God only when the one who claims to be living in him is living the same "kind of life as Christ lived" (1 Jn 2:3-5).

To be in God is to accept Jesus Christ as God's loving presence, speaking continually, through His indwelling Spirit abiding in us, of the Father's infinite love for us, even unto the death of the Cross.

God's life becomes our life in a prayerful experience of God's enormous love that frees us from narcissism and anxieties. The life of Christ within us liberates us to open ourselves to each person we encounter. If in the Old Testament God gave Moses no other name but that He would be discovered as God among His people who were poor, suffering and oppressed, in the New Testament God is love and His Word is again becoming incarnated and brought to new life when two persons love each other unselfishly. No longer is God a far-off power in the heavens. He is speaking His loving presence in His Word, Jesus Christ, who reveals, uncovers, manifests God's liberating power to heal each other's isolation. He releases the power of the Holy Spirit within the context of honest, human self-giving.

> My dear people,
> let us love one another
> since love comes from God
> and everyone who loves is begotten by God and knows God.
> Anyone who fails to love can never have known God,
> because God is love.
> God's love for us was revealed
> when God sent into the world his only Son
> so that we could have life through him;
> this is the love I mean:
> not our love for God,
> but God's love for us when he sent his Son
> to be the sacrifice that takes our sins away . . .
> No one has ever seen God;
> but as long as we love one another
> God will live in us
> and his love will be complete in us.
> We can know that we are living in him
> and he is living in us
> because he lets us share his Spirit . . .
> God is love
> and anyone who lives in love lives in God,
> and God lives in him (1 Jn 4:7-13, 16).

Jesus is the visible manifestation that God is love. We cannot accept Him as God's Word or keep His commandment—to love one another as He has loved us (Jn 15:12), unless we have first surrendered in trust to His loving presence, *wording* within us God's personal love for each of us as individuals. The Spirit of Jesus reveals this loving presence of Jesus always ready to die for *me*. St. Paul well experienced the healing power of Jesus's love for him individually.

> The life I now live in this body,
> I live in faith: faith in the Son
> of God who loved me and who sacrificed
> Himself for my sake (Ga 2:20).

In the light of experiencing the love of Jesus for us individually, then can we transform our lives into loving lives toward all men. ". . . and the reason He died for all was so that living men should live no longer for themselves, but for Him who died and was raised to life for them" (2 Co 5:15).

AN EARTH GOD

In Western Christianity we have worshiped a *Sky God*. He was *up there,* in Heaven, looking down in an immutable, detached way. His Son came down from Heaven and spoke words that, if lived by as a moral code, would merit Heaven for us. He performed miracles and great healings, but above all, He rose from the dead, thus proving He was also a part of the Sky God. He left this world to return to Heaven, but He will come back again in glory.

We have forgotten the Earth God. He is not powerful,

but gentle. He is found in earth's situations. He is most present when He speaks His Word of suffering compassion in Jesus Christ. Jesus Christ is God-Man. But He reveals this to the weak and unworldly children who are called into His Kingdom. Such inhabitants do not prove that Jesus is God. He reveals this in an experience when they become "poor in spirit." Jesus progressively reveals to us the Father as we experience in prayerful communion with His Holy Spirit that God's love for us is an emptying love.

And as we encounter the gentle God, ever so quietly working as soft rain to remove the hardness of our hearts, Jesus Christ, His revealing Word, releases a similar, godly power within us to be emptying in our love. When the seed, God's Word, Jesus Christ, falls into the soft, empty, dark earth of our hearts, it splits into powerful energies that go through our being, transforming us into new creatures.

Jesus becomes on the Cross the full presence of God, the Earth God. It is in the power of stripped and poured out humanity that Jesus proves the power of God's love for us.

Elie Wiesel, the survivor of Auschwitz, in his novel *Night,* describes how the Nazi SS guards hanged two Jewish men and a youth in the presence of the whole camp. As the other prisoners watched the men die quickly, they writhed in pain when they saw the lingering youth, suffering still for a half-hour in the noose.

> "Where is God? Where is he?" someone asked behind me. As the youth still hung in torment in the noose after a long time, I heard the man call again, "Where is God now?" And I heard a voice in myself answer: "Where is he? He is here. He is hanging there on the gallows . . . "[14]

Where is God today? How can we find Him in our jungled cities, polluted oceans, desert woods? He is found, as always: Love poured out unto death, hanging on a cross for me! Yet this Word of God speaks only to the broken in heart, those who cry out to see God's face again. Jesus dying becomes God's spoken Word to us. But only a seeking, prayerful, listening heart can understand what God's Word is saying.

It is about this Jesus Christ, the image of the gentle, suffering Father God, that we wish to write.

> Do you not see now how God has sown up the foolishness of human wisdom? If it was God's wisdom that human wisdom should not know God, it was because God wanted to save those who have faith through the foolishness of the message that we preach. And so, while the Jews demand miracles and the Greeks look for wisdom, here are we preaching a crucified Christ; to the Jews an obstacle that they cannot get over, to the pagans madness, but to those who have been called, whether they are Jews or Greeks, a Christ who is the power and the wisdom of God. For God's foolishness is wiser than human wisdom, and God's weakness is stronger than human strength (1 Co 1:20-25).

CHAPTER 3

JESUS CHRIST — *EBED YAHWEH*

The author, Ken Kesey, in his story, *One Flew Over The Cuckoo's Nest,* gives us a powerful contrast of two characters. Big Nurse, working in the psychotic ward, is a big woman, strong, capable, domineering. She manipulates human beings as though they were machines and is in conflict with off-the-street tough MacMurphy, a patient in the ward. He is the Christ-image in the story. He listens to the other patients and to the doctor in charge. He makes them feel important, possessing a dignity. They respond to his loving concern but in the end MacMurphy's approach costs him his life.

Feodor Dostoievsky wrote a classical novel called *The Idiot*. His biographers tell us he rewrote the ending ten times for he tried to portray the most Christ-like human being he could imagine. Prince Myshkin was considered by many to have been insane, but the children who loved to be near him, loving him, never thought that. After he is declared "sane" and returns from Switzerland to Russia, he continues his Christ-like gentle ways in a society of "normal" people. In the end, the author has his hero return to his form of "insanity."

A MAD GENEROSITY

Jesus came among men, gentle and kind, and told His followers, against the decadent religious leaders of His time, that they were to give away their lives for love of one another. He was the "friend of sinners" and went about doing good. To any sick or disturbed person He brought comfort and healing. He was meek and humble and wanted no part of Caesar's power. The only power He possessed was to love each person who came into His life. He touched the crowds, listened to their anxieties, forgave their sins. He lived only to bring life, and that more abundantly, to all who wanted it. He was total availability to all who needed Him.

He had few disciples because many thought He was *mad*. At least, like the rich young man (Mk 10:17-22), many walked away when He suggested the crazy idea that he who was wealthy should go and sell everything he had, give the money to the poor and follow Him.

He was the most "impractical" person. People were not to worry about what they ate or put on, but they were to seek only the Kingdom of Heaven. But then He didn't have a pillow to put His head on at night. His disciples were to love everyone, even those who hated them. But really! And then He insisted:

> . . . bless those who curse you, pray for those who treat you badly. To the man who slaps you on one cheek, present the other cheek too; to the man who takes your cloak from you, do not refuse your tunic. Give to everyone who asks you and do not ask for your property back from the man who robs you. Treat others as you would like them to treat you. If you love those who love you, what thanks can you expect? Even sinners love those who love them. And if you do good to those who do good to you, what thanks can you expect? For even sinners do that much. And if you lend to those from whom you hope to receive, what thanks can you expect?

> Even sinners lend to sinners to get back the same amount. Instead love your enemies and do good, and lend without any hope of return. . . . Give and there will be gifts for you; a full measure, pressed down, shaken together, and running over, will be poured into your lap; because the amount you measure out is the amount you will be given back (Lk 6:28-38).

His language sounded extravagant, unreal and most impractical. If you had an eye that scandalized you, you were to gouge it out. If you really had faith, you could walk up to a mountain and tell it to jump into the sea and it would do just that.

We were to visit the sick, the lonely, those deadly murderers in prison and tell them that we loved them. We were to give and give, even losing our lives for others. We were to hate our parents, brothers and sisters, and follow only Him. We were to be servants to everyone, washing their feet, binding up their wounds, meeting all their needs.

And all that He asked of His disciples, He did Himself. When He washed the feet of His disciples, He summarized who He was. He was *Ebed Yahweh,* God's servant, suffering for His people.

He was conscious that everything He did came from His Father. He lived only to please Him and bring Him glory. Over and over He confessed that He was nothing while the Father was all. He served the Father, taking nothing unto Himself. In a series of "not I," Jesus asserts His humble role as servant before His Father.

> The Son can do nothing by himself;
> he can do only what he sees the Father doing:
> and whatever the Father does, the Son does too (Jn 5:19).

> I can do nothing by myself;
> I can only judge as I am told to judge ... (Jn 5:30).

> As for human approval, this means nothing to me (Jn 5:41).

> ... because I have come from heaven,
> not to do my own will,
> but to do the will of the one who sent me (Jn 7:16).

> Yet I have not come of myself;
> no, there is one who sent me and I really come from him ... (Jn 7:28).

> ... and that I do nothing of myself:
> what the Father has taught me
> is what I preach (Jn 8:28).

> Not that I care for my own glory,
> there is someone who takes care of that
> and is the judge of it (Jn 8:50).

> And my word is not my own:
> it is the word of the one who sent me (Jn 14:24).

In these statements, Jesus reveals an inner consciousness of His ultimate worth and meaning as a human being that derives from His complete dependence on the Father. There is no vanity or self-seeking in His words or actions. His primal motivation is to serve the wishes of His Heavenly Father. He lives in the presence of His Father. But that Father is constantly working, out of love for Him and the whole universe. "My Father goes on working, and so do I" (Jn 5:17). As the Father loves Him (Jn 15:9) and serves Him in all things, so Jesus loves us and serves us.

THE SUFFERING SERVANT

Jesus and His early disciples were aware that His whole mission in life was to serve the Father's will. But it was clear in the consciousness of Christ made more detailed as He met the unfolding will of His Father each moment of His earthly life, that His service to the Father was a service on behalf of God's people. That service, in God's eternal plan, was to be pushed to such self-forgetting that Jesus would be brought to a free gift of Himself on behalf of the human race. There developed in Jesus an urgency of necessity that eventually His service to mankind would be concretized when He, the Good Shepherd, would lay down His life for all human beings.

The *Kerygma* or preaching of the early Church, as found in the Gospels and Pauline writings, clearly attests to the necessity of Jesus to serve unto humiliating death so that He might enter into glory. On Pentecost, St. Peter preached: "For this reason the whole House of Israel can be certain that God has made this Jesus whom you crucified both Lord and Christ" (Ac 2:36).

Jesus Himself explained patiently to the two disciples on the road to Emmaus:

> You foolish men! So slow to believe the full message of the prophets! Was it not ordained that the Christ should suffer and so enter into his glory? (Lk 24:25-26).

Jesus is presented in the Synoptic Gospels as predicting three times His humiliating death, indicating a certain necessity. In Mark's Gospel Jesus openly preaches: " . . . the Son of Man was destined to suffer grievously, to be rejected by the elders and the chief priests and scribes, and to be put to death, and after three days to rise again. . . " (Mk 8:31). In this context, Peter calls Jesus aside to remonstrate. He did not like such a humiliating plan, for he was expecting Jesus, the Messiah, to be powerful in glory. Jesus called that spirit one of Satan, "because the way you think is not God's way but man's" (Mk 8:33). Evidently such service unto death was a part of God's plan. And if anyone would wish a part with Him, he must go against his selfishness, "lose his life," for in losing one's life for the Gospel he will save it (Mk 8:35).

On another occasion, Jesus repeated the prediction of His suffering and death. But His disciples were arguing among themselves about who was the greatest. "If anyone wants to be first, he must make himself last of all and servant of all" (Mk 9:35). To follow Jesus, who is a servant like a child, one must also be like a child, little in one's self esteem, great in one's loving service toward others.

A third prediction of His humiliating death is followed in Mark's Gospel by another exhortation to suffering out of humble service to one another. James and John, the sons of Zebedee, wanted places of glory next to Jesus. Jesus' answer reveals not only His own mission as suffering servant but that of all called to discipleship.

> . . . anyone who wants to become great among you must be your servant, and anyone who wants to be first among you must be a slave to all. For the Son of Man himself did not come to be served but to serve, and to give his life as a ransom for many (Mk 10:43-45).

It is easy to see in these texts, describing Jesus as suffering servant, the prophetic descriptions in the our songs of Deutero-Isaiah (Is 42:1-9; 49:1-11; 50:4-11; 52:13-53:12).[1]

When Jesus was baptized by John in the Jordan, He humbled Himself to be reckoned among sinners. He heard His Father's voice from heaven: "This is my Son, the Beloved; my favor rests on him" (Mt 3:17). This is the introduction to the first song of the servant of Yahweh:

> Here is my servant whom I uphold,
> My chosen one in whom my soul delights (Is 42:1).

We learn why Jesus gives pleasure to the Father: He has come to serve, not to be served. And His ultimate service will be to surrender His life for all of us to ransom us back from the Kingdom of sin and death (Mt 20:29; Mk 10:45). John the Baptist gives this early Christian teaching when he declares, "Look, there is the lamb of God that takes away the sin of the world" (Jn 1:29). John the Evangelist, who makes much of the parallelism between Jesus and the Passover Lamb, surely must have had in mind the lamb-like characteristics that Deutero-Isaiah attributed to Yahweh's servant.

> Harshly dealt with, he bore it humbly,
> he never opened his mouth,
> like a lamb that is led to the slaughter-house,
> like a sheep that is dumb before its shearers
> never opening its mouth (Is 53:7).

But the Beloved Disciple of Jesus must also have remembered that not only was the Servant of Yahweh, Jesus Christ, a gentle, suffering Savior, but precisely He was serving us by bearing our sins.

> ... he shall divide the spoil with the mighty,
> for surrendering himself to death
> and letting himself be taken for a sinner,
> while he was bearing the faults of many
> and praying all the time for sinners (Is 53:12).

The Suffering Servant Jesus would fulfill the prophecy of Deutero-Isaiah in being a victim on our behalf. He is not a victim of circumstances turned over to the wiles of men who persecuted Him. There is a plan of propitiation for the sins of mankind. He would somehow bear the sins of the world and take them away, as John the Evangelist notes. Isaiah depicted the suffering servant of Yahweh in similar terms:

> And yet ours were the sufferings he bore,
> ours the sorrows he carried.
> But we, we thought of him as someone punished,
> struck by God, and brought low.
> Yet he was pierced through for our faults,
> Crushed for our sins.
> On him lies a punishment that brings us peace,
> And through his wounds we are healed (Is 53:4-5).

THE *KENOSIS* OF JESUS

The outstanding scriptural text that links Jesus' death on the Cross with a humble obedience to the Father is the famous early Christian hymn that St. Paul presents in Ph 2:6-11. Here Paul implies strongly a free choice on the part of Jesus not only to be the servant but also freely to go all the way in obedience to the Father's decree in giving Himself over to death. From such an emptying (*kenosis*), He would be exalted in glory by the Father.

> His state was divine,
> yet he did not cling
> to his equality with God
> but emptied himself
> to assume the condition of a slave,
> and became as men are;
> and being as all men are,
> he was humbler yet,
> even to accepting death,
> death on a cross.
> But God raised him high
> and gave him the name
> which is above all other names
> so that all beings
> in the heavens, on earth and in the underworld,
> should bend the knee at the name of Jesus
> and that every tongue should acclaim
> Jesus Christ as Lord,
> to the glory of God the Father (Ph 2:6-11).

We note in this passage the profession by the Christian community in Jesus' divinity. He was equal with God but He surrendered the glory, the *shekinah,* of God's powerful presence in Him. He did this in order that He could be in all things like us. "God dealt with sin by sending his own Son in a body as physical as any sinful body, and in that body God condemned sin" (Rm 8:3). He was tempted as we are (Heb 4:15). His love for us was so great that there was nothing to distinguish Him from ordinary people. He was a carpenter. He knew hunger, thirst and fatigue. He grew in human knowledge, how to make things, cope with life's problems; above all, how to experience His Father's love in the love He gave to and received from the women and men who came into His life as His friends.

And yet as He grew in consciousness of who He was and what the Father was asking of Him, He continually rejected His own will in complete submission and obedience to His Father's will. He disregarded the shamefulness of the Cross (Heb 12:2), enduring it for love of us and for this reason the Father exalted Him, giving Him the name of Lord of the universe, allowing Him to be called by the name no man could utter, *vere Deus,* Yahweh.

THE LOGIC OF LOVE

I have often asked myself the question: "But why the Cross?" Could God not have been equally pleased that Jesus, as servant, merely lived in that lowly state as man? Even if a blood offering were man's most basic symbol of total giving, could not the human race have been redeemed by one drop from the Lamb of God? Why such a prodigality of emptying, to the point of complete dehumanization? Jesus empties Himself not only of His divine glory but goes further even to emptying Himself of all control over His human existence.

This utter emptying on the Cross was foreseen by the Prophet Isaiah in describing the peak of service on the part of Yahweh's suffering servant.

> Like a sapling he grew up in front of us,
> like a root in arid ground.
> Without beauty, without majesty (we saw him),
> no looks to attract our eyes;
> a thing despised and rejected by men,
> a man of sorrows and familiar with suffering,
> a man to make people screen their faces;
> he was despised and we took no account of him

> and yet ours were the sufferings he bore,
> ours the sorrows he carried.
> But we, we thought of him as someone punished,
> struck by God, and brought low (Is 53:2-4).

But the terrifying sufferings, His service on our behalf, which He underwent, especially in Gethsemane and on Calvary, cannot theologically be understood only by a legalistic atonement theory. According to such thinking, God's justice demanded repayment by the suffering God-Man to atone for man's sinfulness. There must be more that the Word of God reveals to us in deep contemplation of Christ's sufferings, that only His Holy Spirit can reveal far beyond the reach of man's intellect.

Just as our human love knows various degrees of acting out the love we have for another, so Jesus grew in His freedom to surrender Himself completely to the Father. One returns love to the degree that he has been loved. Jesus, in His long hours of solitary communion with the Father, must have received progressively deeper and deeper assurances of the Father's infinite love for Him. If mystics could lose consciousness under the rapture of God's piercing love for them, what must Jesus have experienced as the burning fire of the Father's love for Him poured over Him, filling Him with light, "Light from Light"?

As Jesus experienced in prayerful communion His Heavenly Father's immense love for Him, especially at His Baptism, the forty days alone in the desert, His all-night vigils on the mountaintop, during His public ministry, in the Garden of Gethsemane and in the dying moments on the Cross, He grew in His sensitivity to what love was asking by way of a self-oblation. Much has been written about the psychological development of Jesus' human consciousness.² But because the Gospels are an interpretation of the faith experience of the early Christian community concerning the person, Jesus Christ, we are always left with the uncertainty of knowing, not only what words attributed to Jesus were really His own, but above all of what was His psychological state of consciousness at any stage of His human development.

I believe another theological approach can gain for us also nuanced insights into Jesus' redemptive service on our behalf.

LOVE SAYS SELF-SACRIFICE

It is clear from our human love that the basic level of love and self-sacrifice is to want to do whatever is a clear-cut command or order on the part of the one we love. Jesus throughout His human existence must have been at one with all the pious Jews of His day who strove diligently to return God's love by remembering His commandments and observing them with perfect care. As has been pointed out, He saw during His public life that there was a necessity that He suffer and die. He knew clearly that the Father was calling Him to give up His life for our sakes. And yet obeying His Father's commands was no little sacrifice as His agony in the Garden proves.

> 'Father,' he said, 'if you are willing, take this cup away from me. Nevertheless, let your will be done, not mine.' ... In his anguish he prayed even more earnestly, and his sweat fell to the ground like great drops of blood (Lk 22:42-44).

Still His love prompted Him, within the contexts of the Father's commands, to want to give more. Jesus was sensitive to His Father's loving presence and He desired to be a loving presence to His Father.

In the life of Jesus there were areas of decisions that were free choices made by Him in response to the presence of His Father. These decisions were made sometimes very spontaneously, sometimes with reflection, sometimes in deep, silent prayer. Here we see a more delicate discernment of the will of His loving Father. Not only does Jesus seek to do whatever His Father would command Him to do, but He seeks to act out His return of love by being sensitive to seek in all things to do the slightest wish of the Father expressed in the human situation. It requires greater love, delicacy and discernment to ask what is the wish of the Father in this or that circumstance of the life of Jesus than merely to seek to fulfill the great commands of the Father. For this He moved under the power of the Spirit in greater submission and surrender.

Yet Jesus grew also in going beyond the wishes of the Father to seek in all things to please Him. Even in human love we can bring ourselves from time to time to forget ourselves and, in a burst of self-sacrifice for the one we love, we can "improvise" some gift that costs us a price in sacrifice to "flesh" out our love. The love is there, within our hearts. We made a sacrifice, freely chosen, under no obligation through an expressed command or even a wish on the part of the one we love. Jesus Christ, who had experienced in His humanity the love of the Father as no other person on the face of the earth had, sought to please His Father. He wanted to please Him, make Him happy who gave all things to Him. And so Jesus could say, but, more importantly, could live according to these words:

> ... he who sent me is with me,
> and has not left me to myself,
> for I always do what pleases him (Jn 8:29).

Much in the life of Christ, especially in the terrifying sufferings in His passion and death, can be explained in His free choices to imitate the outpouring love of total self-giving of the Father to His Son. I like to call it "creative suffering." It is what keeps love alive. It is fire touching dry wood and making it turn into fire also. Jesus, loved by the Father infinitely, was being driven in His human consciousness, not by any obligation, but by the consuming desire to take His life in His hands and give it back to His beloved Father. In a way we could say that Jesus, given who He was, the Word of the Father made flesh, "had" to pour Himself out or He would have done psychic and spiritual harm to His nature. In emptying Himself by free choices to suffer more and more, Jesus was becoming the image of His Heavenly Father. He was becoming the Word, God's presence of an infinite love that goes all the way, even unto death, speaking to us all that for each of us God the Father dies in His perfect image.

The suffering servant now becomes better understood. There is light in the darkness of Jesus' *kenosis*. It is not just that He *had* to suffer and die in order to save us from eternal death. Throughout His whole life Jesus freely chooses, when there were possibilities, to descend into the heart of man who was lost. He chooses to descend into the suffering, dying heart of humanity. He freely wishes to become the poorest of the poor, the loneliest of all abandoned human beings. His love for the Father burns so strongly within Him that He will go into the dregs of humanity and desire to become a part of the lowest of the lowliest. As the Prophet Isaiah foretold, He wills to be crushed as a worm beneath the cruel heel of this world that crushes so many other men and women as very worms and not human beings. He freely wills, by a human choice, to taste every ingredient in the bitter chalice that the world, in which the mystery of evil rules, can press to human lips.

There is no constraint in these details. One way is as good as the other as far as the Father goes. His commands and wishes only lead Jesus to this higher perfection of becoming the perfect mirror of the Heavenly Father's complete emptying of Self on our behalf. The Father waits on the free choices of His Son and He becomes surprised, pleased, happy because His beloved Son does whatever pleases the Father. And the Father is pleased because in His infinite wisdom He Himself would have chosen such signs of complete emptying even unto the last drop of blood, if He had a body, if He could speak in human language of suffering unto physical death. But He has a body! He has a physical presence in His Word made flesh. It is the Father who is speaking to each of us in the torn, mangled body of Jesus hanging on the Cross, yelling out in the agony of being abandoned by the Father who loved Him so much. "See, I have branded you on the palms of my hands" (Is 49:16).

LOVE UNTO DEATH

Can we not say, therefore, that Jesus, becoming the suffering servant of Yahweh, freely wants to suffer and be poured out as spilt wax only because He wanted His human mind to be the perfect reflection of the Divine Mind? His human consciousness was to become one with the consciousness of the Father. Jesus in His service to the world, entering into the very depths of sin and death and utter emptiness of self, was choosing humanly to be like God. It was the most perfect plan of imaging the eternal love of the Father for you and me. We have no other way of knowing the Father but through the Son. Here we have the perfect expression in human language of the very being of God.

If God appears as Love in the manger at Bethlehem, how much more does He appear as Love in the stark poverty, humiliations and contempt of the Cross? This act of freely choosing to be one with the sinful humanity to receive the penalty for their sins in the most dramatic emptying, the *kenosis* to the death of the Cross, is the most graphic act of loving service towards all of us human beings.

We read in the Epistle to the Hebrews:

> During his life on earth, he offered up prayer and entreaty, aloud and in silent tears, to the one who had the power to save him out of death, and he submitted so humbly that his prayer was heard. Although he was Son, he learnt to obey through suffering; but having been made perfect, he became for all who obey him the source of eternal salvation and was acclaimed by God with the title of high priest of the order of Melchizedek (Heb 5:7-10).

When Jesus hung on the Cross, as reported by Mark's Gospel (undoubtedly one of the earliest accounts given in the Christian community), He screamed out: "My God, my God, why have you deserted me?" (Mk 15:34). The emptying of the Suffering Servant of Yahweh had reached its peak. God was being manifested for each of us as Love, perfect in His Self-surrender. "A man can have no greater love than to lay down his life for his friends" (Jn 15:13). And we might add: "Nor can God!" God reaches the peak of speaking His Word. He can be no more present as Love than in His Image, Jesus Christ, poured out on the Cross, even to the last drop of blood, made sin, rejected and outcast.

Jerusalem, Jerusalem, you that kill the prophets and stone those who are sent to you! How often have I longed to gather your children, as a hen gathers her chicks under her wings, and you refused! (Mt 23:37).

Jesus had said, "The Father loves me because I lay down my life in order to take it up again. No one takes it from me; I lay it down of my own free will . . . " (Jn 10:17-18). The Father loves Jesus because He lays down His life freely. But this love is so great for Jesus because Jesus makes concrete in human terms our Father's love for us.

A SUFFERING GOD

If the Father loves Jesus because Jesus makes explicit the Father's love for us, is it too far fetched that the Father also undergoes suffering seeing Jesus freely entering into the pit of darkness of human sinfulness and becoming a part of that? Can we not also accept the Father as a suffering servant on our behalf?[3] It is true that the Father does not suffer physically since only Jesus is God-Man. But how can the Word serve by suffering for us human beings and the Mind that speaks that Word remain unmoved?

Love cannot remain uninvolved in the sufferings of the one loved. The Father must be in His Word. The Word has meaning only because He is the exact Image of the Father who is communicating Himself in His Word.

Gerald Vann, O.P. makes a good observation in discussing how God can sorrow with us.

> But in the life of God there are no events; God has no history. Eternity is not an endless line running parallel with the line of time; it is a point; and what to us is past or future

is as much present to eternity as is the actual moment we are now living. . . . Thus the very immutability of God is not a denial of his involvement in the sorrows of these present times, but a triumphant vindication of it. Of the human body of Christ you can say that first it suffered, and then it was glorified and made glad; but throughout that temporal sequence the Godhead remains unchanged, and unchanged precisely in its knowledge and willing of, and its will to share in, that which Christ on the Cross took to himself and made his own and in his glorification turned into glory.[4]

FOR ME HE DIES

Jesus could have suffered and died but He becomes servant to me and you when we open to His burning love for us. When we realize, through His Holy Spirit, that He gives to us only because the Father glorifies Him, that He is always the Father's Word, serving the Father to reveal His great love for us, then His true service becomes effective. The Father is always speaking His Word. Jesus is always loving us unto death. He is now present in our lives with that same dynamic, eternal love that He had when He died to serve us. In prayer, especially in Eucharistic communion, I can realize with St. Paul: "For me He dies!" Such an experience leads me into the awesome presence of the Heavenly Father as perfect holiness, beauty and love. I realize that I am *now* being loved by my infinitely loving Father through the service of the Suffering Servant of Yahweh, Jesus Christ.

Such a healing of our loneliness and self-absorption bursts the bonds that hold us imprisoned in our narcissistic prison. It begins a transformation of our lives which is a process shown by service to others.

... and the reason He died for all was so that living men should live no longer for themselves, but for Him who died and was raised to life for them (2 Co 5:15).

SO AS TO LIVE FOR OTHERS

I can argue that the Heavenly Father will love me if I am like Jesus in all things and especially in sharing somewhat in the mystery of His self-emptying. I would be pleasing to the Father if I were like Jesus who is like the Father. But I cannot be God's Word of self-emptying in order to serve except in the context of serving my nearest neighbor.

But it must be a process that goes beyond a syllogism. Only in prayer can I experience God's Word speaking to me quietly and deeply of God's presence as suffering love. Jesus sheds His blood and I am redeemed by His blood. But this is a discovery in prayer that the Spirit gives me. I begin to realize redemption is not a static, objective, legal moment in which Jesus dies for my sins and those of the whole world. Each day in prayer we can discover afresh that He is again and again serving us out of love, always now, yet always the same as then, always new and yet never changing. And He does still wash our feet; He bears willingly the Cross, dies on it, wants to embrace whatever will touch us and convince us, through "faith in the Son of God who loved me and who sacrificed Himself for *my* sake" (Ga 2:20).

As we experience this love, so like Jesus, we will *want* to live lives of emptying of self and living *for* others in service to the first person who enters our life. God is calling us to let His serving Word go among men, localizing His loving presence through you and me.

I take a ride on the New York subway. I look into the face of the son of man, made to God's Image—Jesus Christ. That is a face filled with tenseness. That man or woman worries whether some violence will hit him before he reaches the relatively safe sanctuary of the home. I see a face haggard with weariness, dull with boredom. A tragic, despairing look, furtively shifting from person to person or buried in the newspaper. There are the lines of fear deeply etched in that face that rarely softens into a warm smile.

To look on the face of the son of man is to see a holy face. It is to see the face of *the* Son of Man Himself, Jesus Christ. The image is defaced. Its beauty can be restored only by godly love shining upon its darkness and bringing it into the glorious light of God's presence. Jesus, the *Ebed Yahweh,* lives in us, loves in us and wishes to serve His broken brothers and sisters through us.

Jesus wishes to be God's presence, as spoken, serving Word through us. He asks us to wash each other's feet.

> If I then, the Lord and Master, have washed your feet, you should wash each other's feet. I have given you an example so that you may copy what I have done to you. I tell you most solemnly, no servant is greater than his master, no messenger is greater than the man who sent him. Now that you know this, happiness will be yours if you behave accordingly (Jn 13:14-16).

Loving, humble service to anyone, especially to the least and the smallest, the oppressed and the fearful, the lonely and the depraved, is the sign that Jesus is Lord and is redeeming us by freeing us to become the focus of God's Word, revealing a Father who suffers as He serves to bring us into happiness.

As the Father spoke to Jesus during His lifetime these beautiful words from Micah, so Jesus, the Suffering Servant, still suffering as God's loving Word in our lives, speaks them within our heart. Let us go forth to love and serve each as Jesus does.

> . . . this is what Yahweh asks of you:
> only this: to act justly,
> to love tenderly,
> and to walk humbly with your God (Mi 6:8).

CHAPTER 4

THE KINGDOM OF GOD IS NEAR

Jesus came among us not only to tell us about God but also to actualize God among us by His actions. What is God like? He is like Jesus. The authority with which Jesus taught His listeners about His Heavenly Father convinced those who accepted Him that He knew the nature of the Father. When Jesus began His preaching, His primary message revolved around the Kingdom of God. His disciples believed that not only did He know what the nature of that Kingdom was but also He was bringing that Kingdom about.

But His teaching about God's Kingdom was so different from what His contemporary Jews expected it to be. They all too easily forgot the suffering servant theme in Deutero-Isaiah. They were really not, therefore, too enthusiastic, as Peter, James and John showed, to follow a King who had to suffer and die in order to enter into His glorious kingdom. Above all, they wanted power and glory, the first seats of honor in the Kingdom, and not to embrace humiliations, poverty, humble service to the least.

If the Kingdom message is so central to the Gospel, we must understand what Jesus understood by it. A. Whitehead claimed that Jesus' message was very quickly distorted when Christianity was officially accepted as the religion of the Roman Empire.

When the Western world accepted Christianity, Caesar conquered.... The brief Galilean vision of humility flickered throughout the ages, uncertainly. In the official formulation of religion, it has assumed the trivial form of the mere attribution to Jews that they cherished a misconception about their Messias. But their deeper idolatry of fashioning of God in the image of the Egyptian, Persian and Roman imperial rulers was retained. The Church gave unto God the attributes which belonged exclusively to Caesar.[1]

A FALSE KINGDOM

Without a doubt we have fashioned a faulty idea about Jesus' message of God's Kingdom. If Jesus reveals to us God and we know already that God is an omnipotent, all-knowing God, absolute in power and glory, then Jesus must be a King of power and glory. So goes our thinking. He will come again in glory to raise us up to share in His power and glory. The Jews before the time of Jesus could perhaps be excused for their distorted views of God's Kingdom that would be restored when the Messiah came. But we have no excuse except our own yielding to the spirit of the world, to "carnal" thinking and our refusal to accept the true message that Jesus preaches about the Kingdom of God.

In the Old Testament, God's Kingdom is spread over the whole universe (Ps 103:19) and is everlasting in power and glory (Ps 145:11-13; Ws 6:4; 10:10). To the "Son of Man" God gives His Kingdom.

> On him was conferred sovereignty,
> glory and kingship,
> and men of all peoples, nations and languages became his servants
>
> (Dn 7:14).

Jesus did not preach His doctrine, therefore, in a vacuum. He was speaking to a people who understood already the imagery of God's Kingdom. God possessed a kingship (*malkuth* in Hebrew). He was sovereign and ruled over Israel with absolute power and might. His kingship and dominion are now being exercised over His People.

> Yours, Yahweh, is the greatness, the power, splendor, length of days, glory, for all that is in the heavens and on the earth is yours. Yours is the sovereignty, Yahweh; you are exalted over all, supreme. Riches and honor go before you, you are ruler of all, in your hand lie strength and power; in your hand it is to give greatness and strength to all. At this time, our God, we give you glory, we praise the splendor of your name (1 Ch 29:11-13).

The Jewish people gradually added the apocalyptic element through Iranian influences and Jewish expectations for the restoration of the Kingdom of David by the Messiah. The apocryphal writings, especially the book of Enoch, well-known in northern Galilee, with Enoch as the Son of Man who is foreseen as exalted in glory by Yahweh, prepared the listeners of Jesus to expect a preacher of an eschatological order to come, who himself would enter into the fullness of glory in the "last days."[2]

THE PREACHING OF JESUS

It is difficult for us to appreciate the impact that Jesus' preaching of the Kingdom had on the various people who listened to His words. John the Baptist came as the last of the Prophets. He confessed he was merely a voice crying in the wilderness that God's chosen People should be repentant. His austerity of attire, diet and message stirred up his listeners to a fear before the wrathful. Yahweh of the Old Testament. He baptized with water but Jesus would baptize with the Holy Spirit (Ac 1:5).

'John's baptism,' said Paul 'was a baptism of repentance; but he insisted that the people should believe in the one who was to come after him—in other words, Jesus' (Ac 19:4).

Jesus, like John the Baptist, preached repentance. But He also preached a message of "good news" (*besorah* in Hebrew) to all classes of people. God's wrath is not the message, but rather the in-breaking of the Father's tender love for each individual.

After John had been arrested, Jesus went into Galilee. There he proclaimed the Good News from God. 'The time has come,' he said, 'and the kingdom of God is close at hand. Repent, and believe the Good News' (Mk 1:14-15).

The "good news" was not only that God was a loving Father of infinite mercy, forgiving each person his sins, bringing healing love to the lonely and desolate, hope to the hopeless, but that the "in-breaking" of God's energies of love into human lives was being at that moment effected by this man Jesus of Nazareth.

The Pharisees and Scribes and those taught by them wanted signs of power and glory that would tell them of the coming of God's Kingdom. Asked by the Pharisees when the Kingdom of God was to come, he gave them this answer, 'The coming of the kingdom of God does not admit of observation and there will be no one to say, "look here! Look there!" For, you must know, the kingdom of God is among you' (Lk 17:20-21).

They wanted signs to be sure that they would recognize the great coming of the Kingdom. Jesus is saying that the Kingdom has already burst upon them. When he drove out devils, this was a sign if they had eyes to see. "But if it is through the finger of God that I cast out devils, then know that the kingdom of God has overtaken you" (Lk 11:20).

The disciples of Jesus were to cure the sick and say, "The kingdom of God is very near to you" (Lk 10:9).

The Scribes and Pharisees, like Saul himself before his conversion, found something very dangerous about this man Jesus and His talk of the Kingdom. If the Kingdom of God is already here, unseen by signs, growing in a mysterious way that is outside of any "legal" control, of what purpose is now their religion of ritualism and externalism? Little by little they began to see that this man Jesus was claiming, not that He was the King of the Kingdom, but that He was the presence of God's "dynamic" power and force, bringing about new, life-giving relationships directly with God.

BECOMING LITTLE LIKE A CHILD

Jesus insisted that only those could receive the Kingdom of God who had the qualities of a child (Mk 10:15; Lk 18:17). Jesus was demanding a conversion of heart, a becoming little and humble, receptive to God's activity in their lives, otherwise the Kingdom that was before their very eyes would not be seen by them.

> 'I tell you solemnly, unless you change and become like little children you will never enter the kingdom of heaven. And so, the one who makes himself as little as this little child is the greatest in the kingdom of heaven' (Mt 18:3-4).

A child who in his "littleness" cries out in utter dependence on others around him for continued growth in life becomes the model for those who wish to enter into God's Kingdom. It is not only a physical poverty, which in itself has nothing of value, but it is a psychic and spiritual poverty that recognizes the absolute sovereignty of God.

> 'How happy are you who are poor: yours is the kingdom of God . . .' (Lk 6:20).

> 'How happy are the poor in spirit; theirs is the kingdom of heaven . . .' (Mt 5:3).

Such an interior poverty is the development of the *anima,* the feminine quality in each human person, to become empty of self-power and openly receptive to God's loving "in-breaking." To such humble and poor ones God reveals Himself.

> I live in a high and holy place, but I am also with the contrite and humbled spirit, to give the humbled spirit new life, to revive contrite hearts (Is 57:15).

Mary, the Mother of God, is the model Christian and the first of the little ones of God's chosen People to receive His Kingdom. She speaks of God's love and mercy shown to the lowly and humble. (Lk 1:47).

> My soul proclaims the greatness of the Lord and my spirit exults in God my saviour; because he has looked upon his lowly handmaid (Lk 1:46-47).

God will enter into an active relationship of comforting those who mourn. He will show mercy to the merciful. The pure of heart shall see Him. He will call the peacemakers His own children. The Kingdom of Heaven is given to those who suffer persecution on behalf of God. They are to rejoice and be glad for a great reward will be given them (Mt 5:6-12; Lk 6:21-23).

A METANOIA

Jesus preached a turning away from one's self-absorption to turn totally to God. This repentance that Jesus preached is a gift that God gives to those who earnestly go out of self to seek God. It does not consist in certain rituals or things done. It is primarily a turning within so as to effect an inner revolution. Man must be "reborn" of the Spirit that Jesus will send him.

> I tell you most solemnly,
> unless a man is born from above,
> he cannot see the kingdom of God.
> ... unless a man is born through water and the Spirit,
> he cannot enter the kingdom of God ... (Jn 3:3, 5).

This conversion is a "losing" of one's life, a decentration away from the false *ego*, to surrender completely to God as the inner, directing force in one's life. The seed has to die of its own self-containment and then it will bring forth new life, a hundredfold (Jn 12:24-25). It is a movement, a slow process whereby God becomes the revolving axis in one's life. It is an enlightenment that is given by God to those who open up as earth to receive God's Word. It not only shows us the meaninglessness of worldly, self-centered values but it also reveals the joy of surrendering to God's holy will in all decisions. The enlightenment continues to create in us new depths of awareness of our own spiritual impoverishment that feeds us with a burning yearning to live by God's desires.

The powerful symbols that Jesus used to describe the transforming element in this conversion of the heart evoke a response in His listeners to unite the forgotten *feminine* side in all of us with the *masculine*. Going into the dark womb and being reborn by God's Spirit, the seed falling into the dark hiddenness of vast, enriching potential of mother earth, suggests the need on our part to activate the feminine principle in us that brings us into direct contact with the dark mysteries of God working within the depths of our being.

THE MYSTERY OF THE SEED

The Kingdom of God comes about mostly when man is not the aggressor, the powerful one who *makes* the Kingdom possible, but when he learns to be docile and gentle before God's loving initiative. Jesus spoke about the Kingdom of God by using parables. His style of teaching by means of parables was a literary form that was well developed in the Old Testament and especially in rabbinic literature.[3] He used it, not to confuse His listeners, but rather to stir their interest and curiosity and thus force them to apply the key point of the story fo their own personal life toward a moral decision, a conversion. For one who is hard of heart, the parable will be meaningless. For the listener who is sincere and open, like well prepared earth, the parable will be the occasion to experience already the fulfillment of the story in his personal life.

One of Jesus' most basic parables that illustrates not only how He taught but how, in the living out of the experience talked about, His listeners would *know* by insights of untold richness, what He was telling, is the parable in Mark's Gospel about the sower who sowed some seed (Mk 4:3-20). A well known process that all human beings had some experience of: planting some seed into the earth and the growth process unto varying degrees of fruition—is presented to His hearers. Yet Jesus is speaking also of a spiritual, invisible growth process that takes place unseen to human eyes.

He says that we receive the Word of God with varying dispositions. Some of us have hearts that resist God's inbreaking presence. The Word of God is present but we are totally "hardened" in heart, absent to His presence. Others of us fail to continue to receive His activating force and, like rocky soil, we allow amidst trials the tender beginnings of our surrender to God to dry up. The thorny ground typifies those of us who allow ourselves to become attached to the things of this world. God's presence, that once was vivid and according to which we lived, now is clouded over by self-seeking.

Not only does He describe various degrees of positive cooperation on our part, to produce a yield of thirty, sixty and a hundred times more than what was planted in our hearts but He also points out in the verses that follow (vv 26-29 which should logically form a whole with the above parable) that the seed unfolds and grows quietly, independently of our knowledge and observation. God's "dynamic" or inner energy is released and does its work quietly. Man cooperates in receiving God's Word. But man cannot control the Word's freedom to grow in God's own mysterious, independent way.

God's Kingdom grows mysteriously within man. Man cooperates in his desire to surrender to God's presence in his life. But the power of growth, the fruits are from God's loving Spirit. We become Christians living dynamically God's life of grace within us when we, as little children, are gifted with the realization of our own inability to do anything but to call out for God's healing love.

> Before the world was made, he chose us, chose us in Christ . . .
>
> . . . And it is in him that we were claimed as God's own, chosen from the beginning. . . . (Ep 1:4, 11).

St. Paul goes on to say that salvation is not a reward for the good we have done but it is a gift from God. It is only God Himself who brings us into His Kingdom by giving us new lives in Christ Jesus (Ep 2:8-10).

THE MUSTARD SEED AND THE LEAVEN

Jesus' parables of the Kingdom of God compared to a mustard seed and leaven in dough highlight how a great work comes from a very insignificant beginning. The end result is so much greater than the humble beginning: a little mustard seed, reputed in Palestine to be the smallest of seeds, grows into a large tree. A bit of leaven in dough raises the whole batch to become bread for hundreds of hungry persons. Jesus tells us that God's Kingdom comes about in insignificant, unspectacular circumstances. God's "enzymic" love works slowly, unseen by human eyes, revealed only to the "pure of heart."

God's actions are operative, His Kingdom is already being effected in a hidden, mysterious manner. This can only be experienced by the one who lives consciously in relationship to God's loving presence. The small mustard seed spreads out its roots and stretches out its branches to become a haven for many birds of the air.

A GREAT TREASURE

The Kingdom of God is not presented by Jesus in any terms of threats but rather as a loving relationship, a state of being in God's life, that is to be desired so eagerly that one would give up everything in order to possess it. To live in God's life, to be directed in all things by God's will, is presented by the Son of God to His listeners as a gift that makes all other desirable objects good only insofar as they aid in obtaining the *one* good.

In comparing the Kingdom to a treasure hidden in a field and found by a man and again as a pearl of great price that a merchant purchases at the cost of selling all he possessed, Jesus is not demanding or commanding what *must* be done. He is pointing out the attractiveness of the gift of the Kingdom and then the joyful response of complete giving in order to possess that gift.

CO-EXISTENCE OF GOOD AND EVIL

Jesus preached the infinite mercy of the Heavenly Father who accepts the Prodigal Son, the harlots, publicans, the Samaritans, sinners of all sorts, in a word, every human being who opens himself to God's healing love. The Pharisees condemned His "liberalism" and freedom to dispense God's forgiveness without demanding the full observance of the Law.

Yet Jesus also preached a judgment doctrine. He described the Kingdom as a community wherein both good and evil persons lived together. But there would be an accounting, a final sifting out of the good, who would enter into the eternal Kingdom, from the evil ones who would be cast into everlasting punishment. This is illustrated by Jesus' parable of the Kingdom likened to a net which gathers fish of every kind, valuable and worthless (Mt 13:47). At the end there will be a selection made. "Again, the kingdom of heaven is like a dragnet cast into the sea that brings in a haul of all kinds. When it is full, the fishermen haul it ashore; then, sitting down, they collect the good ones in a basket and throw away those that are no use" (Mt 13:47-48).

In a similar fashion, Jesus likens the co-existence of the good and the evil within the Church, the Kingdom of God in its earthly stage of development, to a field of wheat and thistles growing together. At the end of the harvest the reapers will sort out the thistles and burn them, but the wheat will be stored in the barn (Mt 13:24-30).

FIDELITY REWARDED

The sifting, with accompanied reward or punishment to the good or the evil, is emphasized by Jesus in His eschatological parables in Matthew's Gospel. The faithful virgins who had trimmed lamps and were waiting for the coming of the Bridegroom entered into the marriage feast while the foolish onew were excluded (Mt 25:1-13).

The faithful servants developed the money given them by the Master while the one who hid his gift in the ground lost it and was cast out into darkness ". . . where there will be weeping and grinding of teeth" (Mt 25:30).

Those who in their lifetime fed the hungry, gave the thirsty to drink, clothed the naked, helped the stranger, visited the sick and those in prison were like the sheep placed at the King's right hand to enjoy eternal glory. The goats were those who failed to show love and compassion to the needy. They were separated on the King's left. "Go away from me, with your curse upon you, to the eternal fire prepared for the devil and his angels" (Mt 25:41).

NOW AND NOT YET

Thus we see the dialectic that Jesus preached concerning the Kingdom. It was already here at hand. Man was being called into this living relationship with God by this man Jesus of Nazareth. His signs: miracles, healings, His parables, but the greatest sign, His very person, were calls at this very moment to a decision. Yet the decision to commit oneself to Jesus and the Kingdom of God was seen as a part of an on-going process of continued growth.

The Kingdom was already being realized and yet its final realization would come only in the future. It is unfolding in our history; yet its fullness lies beyond and outside of history. The Son of Man stands before us at each moment. Yet He will come in full glory in the *Parousia*. The fullness of the Kingdom embraces the entire cosmos that must be brought into completion when Jesus Christ, risen and in glory, will recapitulate all things to God. This is the theme St. Paul often stresses in his epistles, especially those to the Ephesians and Colossians.

The Gospel of St. John stresses the present, realized Kingdom, the Church, that through Baptism, has led its members into the eternal life that is already at hand. Yet John also presents the Kingdom of God, the new life that is already living within the Christian members, as lying in the future. Jesus' work needs to be completed.

> Do not be surprised at this,
> for the hour is coming
> when the dead will leave their graves
> at the sound of his voice:
> those who did good
> will rise again to life;
> and those who did evil, to condemnation (Jn 5:28-29).

John also places the historical Jesus as the inaugurator of the Parousia. "I am going now to prepare a place for you, and after I have gone and prepared you a place, I shall return to take you with me . . . " (Jn 14:2-3).

The "already at hand" and the "not yet" of the Kingdom of God as preached by Jesus cannot be separated. The future is the judgment upon the many "now" moments lived in history before the final day of judgment. Future life in Christ depends on the quality of life in Him lived now in our personal history.

The future also calls us abruptly to the importance of the present moment for dynamic personal decision. The reality of the future metahistorical life in God challenges us pilgrims to live according to "ultimate concern," to use Paul Tillich's term. Life, both now and for eternity, is the same gift of God's presence to us in love. The two are moments in the same growth process.

COMMITMENT TO JESUS

Although Jesus was gentle, non-violent, a lover of all men, especially of the needy and the sinful, yet He made terrifying demands upon those who wished to follow Him. "If any man comes to me without hating his father, mother, wife, children, brothers, sisters, yes and his own life too, he cannot be my disciple. Anyone who does not carry his cross and come after me cannot be my disciple" (Lk 14:26-27).

Jesus insisted that the man who wanted to follow Him but wanted to wait until his father had died should let the dead bury the dead but ". . . your duty is to go and spread the news of the kingdom of God" (Lk 9:60).

Man is free to meet Jesus and accept His invitation to follow Him. The Kingdom is at hand in the person of Jesus. He gently, not with force, invites one to accept Him as Lord in his life. He offers us the occasion to decide in favor of Him, to have "the courage to be," to use Paul Tillich's phrase. It is to accept courage from Christ to be His disciple.

GO, SELL WHAT YOU HAVE

This call to discipleship is poignantly dramatized in the story of the rich young man. He wanted sincerely to possess eternal life. He kept faithful to all the commandments from early childhood. "Jesus looked steadily at him and loved him" (Mk 10:21). Jesus thrilled at his goodness. He probably realized what this young man could have become if . . . Then Jesus invited him to enter into a greater, more intense love relationship with Him.

> 'There is one thing you lack. Go and sell everything you own and give the money to the poor, and you will have treasure in heaven; then come, follow me.' But his face fell at these words and he went away sad, for he was a man of great wealth (Mk 10:21-22).

Jesus was challenging him to give up his identity that he found in his riches and, by becoming poor, to find his true self in a total dependence upon Him. The paradox of becoming poor in order to become truly rich in Jesus was incomprehensible. For a brief moment he stood on the brink of an eternal decision: to choose to believe and live as though this man Jesus had a very special relationship to the Kingdom of God or to believe that money and the possessions of this world made up that Kingdom. "But his face fell at these words and he went away sad, for he was a man of great wealth" (vs. 22).

Martin Buber had once said: "And if there were a devil, it would not be one who decided against God, but one who in eternity came to no decision." Jesus was inviting the young man to make a decision. But he walked away, unable to make the radical choice of Jesus and the Kingdom of God over himself and the riches of this world.

Jesus spoke then on the dangers of attachments to riches. When the Apostles wondered who, then, would be saved, Jesus told them that to follow His demands in order to possess the Kingdom is utterly impossible for man, but not for God. ". . . because everything is possible for God" (vs. 27).

Jesus spoke of the primacy of seeking the Kingdom of God above all other pursuits. If one's eye was a source of scandal or obstacle, preventing him from entering the Kingdom, then he was to gouge it out (Mk 9:43-47; Mt 18:8-9; 5:29-30).

A NEW STYLE OF LIFE

Jesus was insisting that what was impossible to man was possible to God. And so He challenged His disciples to live a new type of life since they were already in the Kingdom. As Jesus showed no violence but only love unto death for others, so those living in the Kingdom were to turn the other cheek. They were to give not only the shirt off their back if asked for it but also their coat. They were to go an added mile when asked to accompany one in need for one mile. Give, He said, and never expect a return. Love all, even enemies (Mt 5: 39-48; Lk 6:27-38). For as the Heavenly Father is perfect, so we must strive to be perfect.

Are we to dismiss these commands as so much Oriental hyperbole? Jesus was a teacher relaying an urgent message to simple, unsophisticated people. He was giving them some concrete examples of ways the children of the Heavenly Father acted and reacted to various human situations. It is because of God's newness of life within the re-born Christian that the follower of Jesus Christ can live a life that is utter nonsense to the worldly-wise. He bestows upon the Christians, through Baptism and especially Holy Eucharist, His Spirit who makes it possible not only to be called children of Abba, Father (Rm 8:15; Ga 4:6) but to live consistently as children of God and brothers and sisters to each person encountered.

A FAITH RESPONSE TO JESUS

Entrance into the Kingdom relationship with God as sovereign begins with an act of faith. Jesus not only announces the Good News that the Kingdom is at hand in this moment, but also reveals that acceptance and commitment to His person is essential to possessing the Kingdom. Faith is God's gift allowing one to accept God's loving presence in Jesus Christ. Because man's fulfillment lies in the way of the cross, persecution and scandal in order to live a constant response to God's will made known through the Spirit of Jesus, his response to Jesus is an on-going process both in this life and in the next.

It is Jesus' gift of the Holy Spirit that guarantees to Christians a presence of Jesus more intimate than that which He possessed during His earthly existence. Jesus and the Father come and dwell within the Christians (Jn 14:23). "And know that I am with you always; yes, to the end of time" (Mt 28:20).

THE BODY OF CHRIST

The Christian does not live only an individual, personal relationship with Jesus, the Heavenly Father and their Spirit of love but he communicates in love that life of the Kingdom within him outwardly to his fellow human beings. God's Kingdom is to come also in the union of all men in Jesus Christ, modeled on the unity and diversity of the Trinity and that Trinitarian life living within each Christian.

That is a living reality, "already now" among Christians (Mt 18:20). The Church is made up of such members through whom the Spirit of Jesus flows as living water, cleansing, binding up together into one Body (Ep 4:4). But the "not yet" is the Church that is in process of becoming more fully realized. It is for this that Jesus prays in His Last Supper Discourse:

> May they all be one.
> Father, may they be one in us,
> as you are in me and I am in you,
> so that the world may believe it was you who sent me.
> . . . With me in them and you in me,
> may they be so completely one

> that the world will realize that it was you who sent me,
> and that I have loved them as much as you loved me.
> . . . I have made your name known to them
> and will continue to make it known,
> so that the love with which you loved me may be in them,
> and so that I may be in them (Jn 17: 21, 23, 26).

The Body of Jesus Christ, the Church, is still in pilgrimage. The Body is growing, extending itself into the hearts of all men through the love of Jesus' Spirit living in the believing Christians (Rm 5:5), who by their loving service seek to build up the Body. The Kingdom of God is already here among us and this is the Good News that Jesus is still preaching to the humble who accept His Spirit. But there is still much darkness surrounding the Light of Christ. Christians still become attached to themselves and to material possessions and ignore, from time to time, the Kingdom of God that is within.

Still they live in constant penitential conversion and Christian hope that what is already within will become more fully manifested both within and without, when the Body of Jesus Christ, the Church, will be synonymous with God's Kingdom. For then God will truly be sovereign and we will belong to Him forever.

> I saw that there was no temple in the city since the Lord God Almighty and the Lamb were themselves the temple, and the city did not need the sun or the moon for light, since it was lit by the radiant glory of God and the Lamb was a lighted torch for it. The pagan nations will live by its light and the kings of the earth will bring it their treasures. The gates of it will never be shut by day—and there will be no night there—and the nations will come bringing their treasure and their wealth.

... The throne of God and of the Lamb will be in its place in the city; his servants will worship him, they will see him face to face, and his name will be written on their foreheads. It will never be night again and they will not need lamplight or sunlight, because the Lord God will be shining on them. They will reign for ever and ever (Rv 21: 22-26; 22: 3-5).

CHAPTER 5

GENTLE JESUS

One of my favorite movies is that of Frederico Fellini, *La Strada*. It is the story of a human brute of animal strength, Zampano, who is a circus strong-man breaking chains. He buys a young girl to accompany his act and to take the collection. She is delicate, like a rare flower that is asked to live in the desert, attacked by the animal coarseness of Zampano. She dies and he finally realizes that he was the cause of her death. For the first time in his life he experiences a gentleness of God's presence in recalling her inner beauty. In a final scene, he staggers drunkenly into the sea, sobbing in repentance. The gentle water washes his coarseness away and restores him to a new human existence.

Prophetic writers like Goethe and Dostoievsky have also described Western man in their Faust and Raskolnikov, redeemed by the insane child-killer Gretchen and the prostitute Sonya. With poignancy we read in *Faust* Goethe's cry for salvation through the feminine:

> Transitory things are symbolical only.
> Here the inadequate finds its fulfillment.
> The not expressible is here made manifest.
> The eternal in woman is the gleam we follow.[1]

In Scripture between the sign of hope that salvation would come from the seed of the woman (Gn 3:15) and the child-bride, Mary, who accepts to become the Mother of Jesus, God-Man, we have a story of God's pursuit of man. The tender gentleness of God's love for man became eclipsed as God's chosen people turned away from Him in their aggressive sinfulness. They projected an image, therefore, of the Sky God, up in the heavens, fearful and revengeful. He led them into violent battles and caused their successes. He was a God of anger and storm, of violence and manipulation. He was a law-maker demanding the fulfillment of every "jot and tittle" with complete obedience.

Many Western forms of Christianity accepted such a portrait of a masculine God, to the loss, as Carl G. Jung has often pointed out, of the feminine polarity. Such an image of God well suited the Western mentality. He is a *doing* God, a powerful creator. He is efficient and strong, orderly, a God of business, of commerce, of owning and possessing, of barter and profit. He is a God of organization, politics, laws, and obligations.[2]

Without the feminine power of contemplation that yields insight rather than material power of possessions, our Western world will soon have to declare bankruptcy. C.S. Lewis cleverly shows, in an essay aptly entitled, "The Abolition of Man,"[3] that our world will be manipulated by a handful of leaders who will treat us, in Kafkasque or Orwellian language as mere "things" if we continue to lose the sense of poetic truth.

When we apply such an approach to Jesus of the Gospels we find many interesting but alarming results that have little to do with the Carpenter of Nazareth. For many today, Jesus is preached according to liberal rationalism, as a humanist who gave us a model of what we can do to better this world. Or in other circles like Jansenism and

Puritanism, the masculine God of the Old Testament brings forth His austere Son, powerful but utterly detached from this material, evolutive world.

Still other Christian pietistic groups create a "sweet" effeminate Jesus who supplies, as Dietrich Bonhoeffer says, an escape for the cowardly. His trenchant words are a stern rebuke to a Western world that seeks to replace the masculine God with a purely feminine one.

> Whenever life begins to become oppressive and troublesome, a person just leaps into the air with a bold kick and soars relieved and unencumbered into so-called eternal fields. He leaps over the present. He disdains the earth; he is better than it. After all, besides the temporal defeats he still has his eternal victories, and they are so easily achieved. Other-worldliness also makes it easy to preach and to speak words of comfort. An other-worldly Church can be certain that it will in no time win over all the weaklings, all who are only too glad to be deceived and deluded, all utopianists . . .[4]

RETURN TO THE ANIMA

We in the West are sensing the need of rediscovering the feminine polarity in our psychic make-up. Science has given us technology through the inductive and deductive rational systems. We have entered into outer space travel that has brought human life to the moon. With our advanced methods in medicine and agriculture we have the means of extending human life and feeding the millions in the third world, of making this a more human planet for all world citizens.

Yet the pollution that comes as the price to be paid for such industry, the wars, the rampant social injustices, poverty and starvation, that not only still exist but are ever increasing, have forced us to go back into our past to find the forgotten feminine corrective. We need to develop the sense of poetry and play, joy and gentleness, to be receptive to the mysterious in love that can be experienced only by humble service. We cry out in our society and in our Christian Churches for a God who is more than powerful—for one who is also gentle, loving, suffering. Our Christianity is demanding that not only we individuals become integrated, healed and whole persons, but that the Jesus we worship and preach to others become also, as the Gospel truly portrays Him to be, a fully integrated person.

THE GENTLE JESUS

Jesus is the full manifestation of God's loving presence among us. He came to correct the distorted view that many of the Jews had of God. In the words of St. Irenaeus of the 2nd century:

> For this is why the Word of God is man, and this is why the Son of God became the Son of Man, that man might possess the Word, receive adoption and become the son of God.[5]

He came to show us what we could become. But He also was the true image in His person and in His message of what God is like. He came to reveal the androgynous nature of God. For God is love and this means to give and to receive love. That God could give love was evident to the Jews of Jesus' time. But that God could be gentle, waiting for our love, suffering when we refused to respond, this was an important revelation made by God's incarnate Word.

For the Christian who believes by faith that Jesus Christ is "truly God, truly man," the gentleness and feminine side of Him shines forth in contrast to the masculine power possessed in His creative omnipotence. St. Tychon of Zadonsk (+ 1783), one of Russia's great "kenotic" saints, beautifully captures the gentle side of Jesus in contrast to His power.

> Listen, my soul: God has come to us;
> Our Lord has visited us.
> For my sake He was born of the Virgin Mary,
> He was wrapped in swaddling clothes,
> He who covers heaven with the clouds
> and vests Himself with robes of light.
> For my sake He was placed in the lowly manger,
> He whose throne is the heavens and whose feet rest upon earth.
> For my sake He was fed with His mother's milk,
> He who feeds all creatures.
> For my sake He was held in His mother's arms,
> He who is borne by the Cherubim
> and holds all creatures in His embrace.
> For my sake He was circumcized according to the law,
> He who is maker of the Law.
> For my sake, He who is unseen
> became visible and lived among men,
> He who is my God.
> My God became one like me, like a man;
> the word became flesh,
> and my Lord, the Lord of Glory,
> took for my sake the form of a servant
> and lived upon earth and walked upon earth
> He who is the King of Heaven.
> He labored, worked miracles,
> conversed with men, was like a servant,

> He who is the Lord of all.
> He was hungry and thirsty,
> He who provides food and drink for all creatures.
> He wept, He who wipes away all tears.
> He suffered and mourned,
> He who is the consoler of all men.
> He consorted with sinners,
> He who alone is just and holy.
> He who is omnipotent toiled
> and had nowhere to lay His head,
> He who lives in light inaccessible.
> He was poor,
> He who gives riches to all men.
> He wandered from town to town and from place to place,
> He who is omnipresent and fills all space.
> And thus for thirty-three years and more
> He lived and labored upon earth for my sake—
> I who am His servant. [6]

Jesus was gentle, not because He did gentle things that were seen by men but because He existed always present to His Heavenly Father. His gentleness was His way of existing in the truth of His Father's awesome transcendence in His life. The Father was greater than He and without the Father the Son could do nothing (Jn 5:30; 14:28). Everything Jesus had, by way of revealed word or power of healing and miracles, came to Him from the Father (Jn 5:20 and passim).

The Father was always working (Jn 5:17) and Jesus was working together with Him. He was not an automaton without free will, but in all things He turned inwardly to find His Father at the center of His being (Jn 14:11). There in the depths of His heart, His innermost consciousness, Jesus touched the Holy. He breathed, smiled, laughed and cried in that holy presence of His infinitely loving Father. All outside creatures, touching Jesus in new, surprising experiences, were received by that delicate, sensitive gentleness in Him as gifts. Absent were the moods of aggressive autonomy and uncontrolled self-indulgence. Jesus was always present to the Father because the Father was always speaking His loving word in Him.

The beautiful words of the poet, Gerard Manley Hopkins, S.J., describe the constant attitude of Jesus-Gift toward His Father, the Giver.

> Thee God I come from,
>   To Thee go.
> All day long I like fountain flow,
>   From Thy hand out,
> Swayed about
>   Mote-like
> In Thy mighty glow.

ALL THINGS HOLY

Wrapt in God's loving presence, Jesus was the gentle servant, receiving His being from the Father and seeking to return Himself completely to the Father in self-surrender. To do the will of the Father was His great delight and Jesus joyfully met each person and each event with the excitement of a child discovering new happenings of beauty.

The many references to nature, to the inanimate and plant and animal worlds around Jesus, tell us of His sensitivity, His gentle receptivity toward the material world. Lambs freshly born, seeds sown in the soft earth, the rain and its cleansing power, the birds that never stored grain into barns, the fox in its den, the grape vines being pruned, the flaming sunset, spangling the west with portents of fair weather, all creatures shouted out to the gentle Jesus that His Father was near, holy and good, beautiful and loving and He too wanted to be beautiful and gentle. The words of the Greek novelist Nikos Kazantzakis, come to mind to express how Jesus heard all beauties of nature speak to Him of God:

> I said to the almond tree: "Speak to me of God,"
> And the almond tree blossomed.[7]

But the children who make up the Kingdom of Heaven experienced Jesus gentle in a special way.

> People were bringing little children to him for him to touch them. The disciples turned them away, but when Jesus saw this he was indignant and said to them, 'Let the little children come to me; do not stop them; for it is to such as these that the kingdom of God belongs. I tell you solemnly, anyone who does not welcome the kingdom of God like a little child will never enter it.' Then he put his arms around them, laid his hands on them and gave them his blessing (Mk 10:13-16).

What gentleness must have been expressed in his loving gaze upon the first disciples, John and Andrew, who met Him at the Jordan and stayed with Him until evening. "Rabbi, . . . where do you live?" (Jn 1:38). There is Jesus' special gentleness toward the impetuous, outspoken Peter, so different from His gentleness toward John the Beloved. And then his gentleness toward Judas! "My friend, do what you are here for" (Mt 26:50).

There is His special gentleness to the broken in body, soul, spirit. It is shown in His compassion as He heals the ruler's son at Cana (Jn 4:46-54), the possessed man in the synagogue (Mk 1:23-28), Peter's mother-in-law (Mk 1:29-34), the lepers, the blind, the paralytics. We see His gentle thoughtfulness toward the widow of Naim:

> When the Lord saw her he felt sorry for her. 'Do not cry,' he said. Then he went up and put his hand on the bier . . . and said, 'Young man, I tell you to get up.' . . . and Jesus gave him to his mother (Lk 7:13-16).

He has pity on the multitudes and feeds them miraculously (Mk 6:34-44; 8:1-10). But He shows a special gentle concern for those mentally disturbed such as the Gerasene demoniac. "Go home to your people and tell them all that the Lord in his mercy has done for you" (Mk 1:19). His affected sternness shown to the Syrophoenician woman must have allowed His gentle kindness to shine forth, encouraging deeper faith in the woman who would not be put off until Jesus had cast out the devil from her daughter (Mk 7:24-30).

He wept over Jerusalem because of the hardness of their hearts.

> Jerusalem, Jerusalem, you that kill the prophets and stone those who are sent to you! How often have I longed to gather your children, as a hen gathers her chicks under her wings, and you refused! (Mt 23:27-38).

He showed His love for the sinner as He gently restored the Samaritan woman (Jn 4:10-26) and the woman caught in the act of adultery (Jn 8:3-11) to a new sense of personal dignity.

He was called a friend of tax collectors and prostitutes by His enemies. Not only does He seek out the repentant sinners and fill them with His peace but He does it often in an engaging manner spiced with a sense of humor. Who can fail to see His playful smile as He looks up into the sycamore tree to call Zacchaeus down to receive salvation? How He smiled at the enthusiastic conversion of his publican host: "Look, sir, I am going to give half of my property to the poor, and if I have cheated anybody I will pay him back four times the amount." For that was why the gentle Jesus had come, "to seek out and save what was lost" (Lk 19:1-10).

GENTLE TO HIS FRIENDS

Such a gentle person as Jesus must have known deep human loves. The multitudes sought Him out for favors and out of curiosity. Some few, Jesus allowed to experience His loving heart, so ready to share Himself with them in deep intimacies of words and silences, looks and touches. He had a special, personal love toward each of His chosen Apostles. "As the Father has loved me, so I have loved you" (Jn 15:9). With tender love He washed their feet (Jn 13:4-11). He gave them His own body and blood that they, eating and drinking, might have His life everlasting. He breathed upon them after His resurrection and gave them His Spirit and commissioned them to forgive sins and heal the sick as He did (Mk 16:16-20).

At the Last Supper He allows John the Beloved to place his head affectionately close to His breast. This same John wrote that he and the other disciples had not only seen the Word who is life but they also had touched Him (1 Jn 1:1).

What warm love He had for His friend Lazarus at whose tomb He wept.

> ... Jesus said in great distress, with a sigh that came straight from the heart, 'Where have you put him?' They said, 'Lord, come and see.' Jesus wept; and the Jews said, 'See how much he loved him!' (Jn 11:13-37).

He loved Lazarus and his two sisters, Mary and Martha, as His intimate friends. He ate at their table, but Mary seemed to have a special sensitivity as she is pictured sitting at His feet, listening to Jesus speak (Lk 10:39). She anoints His feet with the costly ointment in the house of Simon the leper at Bethany (Mk 14:3-9).

Women traveled with Jesus to serve Him, especially some like Mary Magdalene from whom He drove seven demons and Joanna, the wife of Herod's steward Chuza, Suzanna and "several others who provided for them out of their own resources" (Lk 8:2-3). It was probably Mary Magdalene who is depicted as the prostitute who washed Jesus' feet with her tears and wiped them with her luxuriant hair and "covered his feet with kisses and anointed them with the ointment" (Lk 7:38).

Her attachment to the gentle Jesus who brought her interior peace and joy drew her to the side of Mary, Jesus' mother as the virgin-mother and the harlot stood before the dying Jesus who loved them both so differently and yet loved each one uniquely. Mary Magdalene's devotion showed itself in her wild desire at the tomb of Jesus to go and carry His body away. The gentle Jesus dispelled her grief with one simple word: "Mary!" (Jn 20:16). No human being ever pronounced her name as did the risen Jesus for no human person ever knew her and loved her in her heavenly Father's love as did Jesus.

MARY HIS MOTHER

If mothers exert a tremendous influence, far greater than fathers, in shaping the attitudes and character strengths of their children, is it far-fetched to believe that Jesus learned many of His gentle traits that others saw in His conduct toward them from His Mother, Mary? At Bethlehem and at Nazareth during the infancy and early childhood of Jesus, Mary poured out a heart of total love as she lived out her *fiat:* "I am the handmaid of the Lord, . . . let what you have said be done to me" (Lk 1:38).

We learn of her gentle concern for others at the wedding feast of Cana. She anticipates the embarrassment of the newlywed couple by informing her Son, ever so gently: "They have no wine" (Jn 2:3). Sensitive, totally feminine, Mary was open to the needs of all. Her gentle strength is above all portrayed by John the Evangelist as she stood suffering at the foot of the Cross (Jn 19: 25-27). Jesus learned from His mother how to be gentle.

A GENTLE STRENGTH

We cannot forget an important aspect of the gentleness of Jesus that prevented Him from becoming a victim of injustices around Him and that is His anger and severity shown often towards His enemies. As He was able to love strongly because He loved according to the mind of His Father, so He was capable of strong anger according also to the judgment of God. The Father had given Him all right to judge (Jn 5:22). He had "appointed him supreme judge" (Jn 5:27).

He strongly slashes out at the hypocrisy of the Pharisees and Scribes (Lk 11:37-40; Jn 5:37-47; Mt 12:24-25, 31-34). The whole twenty-third chapter of Matthew's

Gospel is a powerful indictment of the teaching classes of the Jews by a very "angry" Jesus. "Hypocrites!" "Whitewashed tombs!" "Serpents, brood of vipers!"

In angry protest He drove the merchants and moneychangers from the Temple precincts (Mt 21:12-13). It was zeal for His Father's house which they had turned into a market place. Yet we never hear of Jesus inflicting any physical harm upon any merchant or upon anyone else throughout His earthly life. Still to those who inflicted great pain and ultimately brought about His death on the cross, He offered a prayer of gentle forgiveness to His Father: "Father, forgive them; they do not know what they are doing" (Lk 23:34).

He turned upon Peter with an angry rebuke that should have frightened him into complete submission. Peter had his own ideas about how Jesus would restore the Kingdom of Israel and the predicted sufferings and death of Jesus were getting just a bit too close to himself. "Get behind me, Satan! You are an obstacle in my path, because the way you think is not God's way but man's" (Mt 16:23). Peter would betray Jesus and yet the gentle Jesus would forgive him. Yet how firmly Jesus attacks Peter for seeking to draw Him away from doing the will of His Father.

AN INNER GENTLENESS

Jesus was the reflection of His Father, full of His grace and glory. The presence of His Father bathed Him in His loving light. He felt this inner, uncreated energy of the Father and His Spirit of love swelling from the depths of His being. Gentleness with Jesus was not something He acquired by studying traits and external actions done by "gentle-men." He could call out with loving compassion to all who were broken in any way, heavily burdened, and He would strengthen them because from His inner depths He was gentle by nature of being one with His Father "... for I am gentle and humble of heart..." (Mt 11:29).

Jesus was gentle in heart because He lived in a continued state of prayerful worship and loving surrender to His Father. Every thought, word and action was in harmony with the will of His Father whom He strove to please in all things. Jesus was gentle because He was free—free to be totally Himself, to be completely human in each situation because He was so totally at one with His divine Father.

> ... on him the spirit of Yahweh rests,
> a spirit of wisdom and insight,
> a spirit of counsel and power,
> a spirit of knowledge and of the fear of Yahweh.
> He does not judge by appearances,
> he gives no verdict on hearsay,
> but judges the wretched with integrity,
> and with equity gives a verdict for the poor of the land.
> His word is a rod that strikes the ruthless,
> his sentences bring death to the wicked.
> Integrity is the loincloth round his waist,
> faithfulness the belt about his hips (Is 11:2-5).

The sign of the Kingdom of God come among us is the gentleness of the lamb before its shearers (Is 53:7). Jesus gentle breaks down the power structures that we build up in our insecurity. He reveals in His gentleness that the awesome, vengeful Yahweh is a sensitive, suffering God. Realizing that God is gentle as Jesus is, we can become joyful, laughing children again. Fear that comes from our anxious lack of true identity is dispelled by the love of God poured out for us on the Cross. The Lamb of God is the sign of God's great power—to pour Himself out on our behalf until the last drop of blood. God conquers us by the gentleness of Jesus. And for this reason His servants will worship the Lamb and the "Lord God will be shining on them. They will reign forever and ever" (Rv 22:4-5) because they will have been gentle as He.

>Happy the gentle;
>they shall have the earth for their heritage (Mt 5:4).

CHAPTER 6

JESUS HEALS

In a scene from the popular musical, *Jesus Christ Superstar,* Jesus finds Himself in a deserted, rocky place. Out of the caves and holes in the rocks, crawl the lepers, the blind and crippled, seeking to touch Him and be healed. Jesus is deluged and sucked down into the mass of broken humanity. As the sick claw at Him, Jesus screams, "It's too much! There are too many of you!"

Jesus the Light came into our darkness. He carried within Himself the fullness of God's life and wholeness. He came among us to share that divine life. He came as the Divine Physician that we might be healed and share in His abundant life. "I have come so that they may have life and have it to the full" (Jn 10:10).

The one great sin for us human beings is to live in the darkness of our own isolated loneliness. We were made for loving union with God and all human beings. But sin forces us to resort to power as the means to move out of our self-absorption. We seek by many so-called sinful actions to powerize ourselves into a proper acceptance by others. Yet pitifully such approaches lead us farther and farther from true love.

Yet Jesus' redemptive power is one of removing our ignorance by giving us through His Holy Spirit an abiding experience of the Heavenly Father's great love. Jesus spoke to those who heard Him during His lifetime on earth and still speaks to us through the Gospel stories. But it was not what He said that touched hearts and healed them. It was His loving presence that could touch the sick and the sinful, that could gaze upon them and mirror for them the infinite love of the Father. He stirred up the imageness of Himself locked in each person whom He met and called it into being. He was the Son of God and He loved the son and daughter of God in each person He met.

> Yes, God loved the world so much that He gave His only Son, so that everyone who believes in him may not be lost but may have eternal life (Jn 3:16).

The human race that sat in darkness saw a great light in Jesus, as the Prophet Isaias had predicted (Is 9:2; Mt 4:16). His revealing presence of God's Word took the form of *teaching* in the synagogues and *preaching* the Gospel of the Kingdom and *healing* all manner of diseases.

> He went round the whole of Galilee teaching in their synagogues, proclaiming the Good News of the kingdom and curing all kinds of diseases and sickness among the people. His fame spread throughout Syria, and those who were suffering from diseases and painful complaints of one kind or another, the possessed, epileptics, the paralysed, were all brought to him, and he cured them (Mt 4:23-34; Mt 9:35).

JESUS DESTROYS SIN

The Good News was that God was preparing His people for the final revelation of His burning love for them. Isaiah and Jeremiah had foretold the new times when tears would be wiped away and sorrow would be no more. God's revealing Love stood before those suffering and was filled with compassion, seeing how they were held in bondage of sin and sickness.

> And when he saw the crowds, he felt sorry for them because they were harassed and dejected, like sheep without a shepherd (Mt 9:36).

The Genesis account describes how through man's body, his spirit was tempted toward independence. Man wanted aggressively to control his life, to be like God. He refused to live on the deep level of interior communion with God by faith, hope and love. He became a slave to his senses. But God sends us His Son to undo the work of Satan. "It was to undo all that the devil has done that the Son of God appeared" (1 Jn 3:8). Jesus was made sin for us (2 Co 5:21).

Matthew's Gospel gives us an inspired exegesis of Is 53:4 when it is written that Jesus "cast out the spirits with a word and cured all who were sick. This was to fulfill the prophecy of Isaiah: "He took our sicknesses away and carried our diseases for us" (Mt 8:16-17).

The prophecy given by Deutero-Isaiah reads:

> And yet ours were the sufferings he bore,
> ours the sorrows he carried.
> But we, we thought of him as someone punished,
> struck by God, and brought low.
> Yet he was pierced through for our faults,
> crushed for our sins.
> On him lies a punishment that brings us peace,
> and through his wounds we are healed (Is 53:4-5).

In Jesus, God forgives all our offenses and cures all our diseases (Ps 103:3). God's mercy that is above all His works (Ps 145:9) becomes incarnated in Jesus of Nazareth. It would be only when He suffers and dies, ignominiously emptied out on the Cross, that Jesus becomes the living Word of God's healing presence among us.

MERCIFUL LOVE OF GOD

But the whole of Jesus' public life was to manifest the tender, merciful love of God for His suffering children. At times Jesus manifests a reticence to demonstrate His power to heal. At other times He appeals to His miracles and healings as signs of His oneness with the Father. These are not weak vacillations in Jesus' character. His primary work, His hour, was to become the fullness of God's communicating, loving presence to mankind. He would not be side-tracked by any vain glory as a miracle worker or healer. He was merely the Word spoken by God.

Yet because He was so much one with the Father, seeing the maimed, the blind, the lepers and the paralytics, the epileptics and the possessed, the sinners bound by hatred for others, by lust and pride, He, as it were, could not but be compassionate, full of mercy and loving as His Father is. Throughout His whole public ministry Jesus imaged His Father's loving concern for His children. He knew what forces of evil were seeking to destroy God's people. And wherever He saw the power of darkness covering mankind, he burned with zeal to bring the light of God's love to destroy the effects of sin.

It was the whole man, body, soul, spirit, that spoke to Jesus. Because His Father was a loving Father, concerned with every facet of man's being, so Jesus was equally touched to see man sick and unhealthy on any level. He came to release the potential for healthy, happy living locked in the depths of each person created by God according to Jesus, the Image of God (Gn 1:26).

Sin brought disease and death into this world but God was Yahweh who always healed His people, provided they lived according to His ways.

> If you listen carefully to the voice of Yahweh your God and do what is right in his eyes, if you pay attention to his commandments and keep his statutes, I shall inflict on you none of the evils that I inflicted on the Egyptians, for it is I, Yahweh, who give you healing (Ex 15:26).

From Scripture we see that God can and does inflict evils upon human beings to draw them back to Him. He is even then a loving Father, disciplining His children. He prunes those whom He loves that they may bring forth greater fruit (Jn 15:1).

> For the Lord trains the ones that he loves and he punishes all those that he acknowledges as his sons. Suffering is part of your training; God is treating you as his sons (Heb 12:6-7).

With St. Paul we profess that all things, even sickness can work unto good for those who love the Lord (Rm 8:28). He prayed three times to be healed of his "thorn in the flesh" and received the answer from Jesus that His grace would be sufficient for him to bear the suffering. He learned in suffering: ". . . when I am weak then I am strong" (2 Co 12:10).

Yet Scripture also teaches us that through Adam's sin,

sin entered into the lives of all men and with sin, also death (Rm 5:12). Sicknesses are a form of incipient death and Jesus came to free us from both sin and death.

> Since all the children share the same blood and flesh, he too shared equally in it, so that by his death he could take away all the power of the devil, who had power over death, and set free all those who had been held in slavery all their lives by the fear of death (Heb 2:14-15)

The many healings of sicknesses and diseases of all kinds that Jesus performed were a sign of the "new age." Man was being restored by Jesus to divine sonship (Ep 1:5). God's children, like His Son, Jesus, would be freed of death and sickness.

IF YOU BELIEVE

But in His healings, Jesus insisted on two conditions. The first element that was present and often expressed in the Gospel accounts of healings is the need of believing in Jesus' power and love to heal the sick persons encountered.

> Have faith in God. I tell you solemnly, if anyone says to this mountain, 'Get up and throw yourself into the sea,' with no hesitation in his heart, but believing that what he says will happen, it will be done for him. I tell you therefore: everything you ask and pray for, believe that you have it already, and it will be yours (Mk 11: 22-24).

Often Jesus drew this faith from the sick. He asks the blind Bartimaeus: "What do you want me to do for you? . . . Go, your faith has saved you" (Mk 10:51). He had the woman with a hemorrhage confess her belief that if she only touched the hem of his garment, she would be cured. ". . . your faith has restored you to health" (Mk 5:34). Jesus cured the leper who returned to thank Him: "Your faith has saved you" (Lk 17:19).

Jesus confessed that He had not found such faith in Israel as He found in the pagan Centurion who believed Jesus could cure his servant. Because of this faith he cured the servant (Mt 8:6-13). Jesus drew deeper faith from the father of the epileptic demoniac who had only asked Jesus to do something to help his son. "Everything is possible for anyone who has faith" (Mk 9:24).

When the Disciples asked Jesus why they were unable to heal the boy, Jesus taught them the necessity of faith in healing.

> Because you have little faith. I tell you solemnly, if your faith were the size of a mustard seed, you could say to this mountain, "Move from here to there," and it would move; nothing would be impossible for you (Mt 17:20).

All things, Jesus said, that one were to ask for in prayer, believing, he would receive (Mt 21:22). He was demanding a faith that is the "evidence of things not seen" (Heb 11:1), a faith in God's loving power to be able and to want to heal all forms of sickness on a bodily or psychical level. Jesus blessed such faith with healings. But where He found this faith lacking, there was no healing. We read that in Nazareth among his own fellow-townsmen He could heal only a few persons because of their lack of faith in Him (Mk 5:25).

Peter and John heal the cripple at the Gate Beautiful near the Temple "in the name of Jesus Christ the Nazarene, walk!" (Ac 3:6). Peter preached that it was not due to any power that he or John possessed but only because of their faith in Jesus. "... it is the name of Jesus which, through our faith in it, has brought back the strength of this man whom you see here and who is well known to you. It is faith in that name that has restored this man to health..." Ac 3:16).

SINS FORGIVEN

The other element in Jesus' healings is tied intrinsically to the first element of faith in Him. To believe in Jesus is to live according to His teachings. He came to free us from sin of which sickness often was a manifestation. He exhorted His followers to pray with complete conviction that they were already receiving what they prayed for, even before there was any external sign. But He puts down as a condition for such conviction that we surrender our lives to Him. We are to live by His Spirit of love and forgiveness.

> And when you stand in prayer, forgive whatever you have against anybody, so that your Father in heaven may forgive your failings too (Mk 11:25).

Because of sin, God permits sickness to show us our weakness, to purify our hearts, to make us trust more totally in Him. God can bring such sickness about in us as long as sin rules in us. Our sinful natures in the majority of cases, as medical experts point out, when the psyche is not in proper relationship with God, are the causes of many psycho-somatic disturbances. Along with faith that Jesus can heal sicknesses, His followers must confess their sinfulness and be converted to God.

This confession is first of all one of recognizing our sinfulness and inability to bring about our own reconciliation with the Father. "Jesus, Son of David, have pity on me" (Lk 18:38). It is the compunction put into our hearts by Jesus' Spirit that allows us to cry out in sorrow and shame with the publican in the rear of the synagogue: "God, be merciful to me, a sinner" (Lk 18:13).

Secondly, we must claim Jesus as sole Lord and believe that He is the Son of God and can do all things. He is the announced Messiah who is coming to bring us into a new creation. "But you . . . who do you say I am?" (Mt 16:16). His followers must not only surrender to His power but to His love that will brook no compromise. To live in Christ Jesus is to deny ourselves, to take up our daily cross of self-renunciation, in order to let Him be supreme in our lives (Mt 16:24-25; Mk 8:3-4, 9:1; Lk 9:23-27).

That is why in Christian healing the first healing is an infusion of faith by the Holy Spirit to believe and trust completely in Jesus, in His love as a true image of the Father's love, to let go of our lives, by removing any deliberate sinful attachments and, more positively, by a childlike abandonment to God's protective love. A deeper healing of our spirit allows us to live Jesus' teaching to seek first the Kingdom of God and all other things, including bodily and psychic health will be added unto us (Lk 12:31). Then Jesus' words will be true:

> Ask, and it will be given to you; search, and you will find; knock, and the door will be opened to you. For the one who asks always receives; the one who searches always finds; the one who knocks will always have the door opened to him (Lk 11:9-10).

Jesus first forgave the sins of the paralytic who was lowered through the roof in order that he might receive his physical healing (Lk 5:18-25). But in the cure of the sick man at the Pool of Bethzatha, John the Evangelist presents to us the early Christian community's teaching on first forgiveness of sins, belief in Jesus and then a healing on the physical or psychic level. "Now you are well again, be sure not to sin any more or something worse may happen to you" (Jn 5:14).

This was the doctrine taught in St. James' epistle that gives the early Christian practice of confession of sins and the prayer of faith for the healing of all sicknesses.

> If any of you is ill, he should send for the elders of the church, and they must anoint him with oil in the name of the Lord and pray over him. The prayer of faith will save the sick man and the Lord will raise him up again; and if he has committed any sins, he will be forgiven. So confess your sins to one another, and pray for one another, and this will cure you (Jm 5:14-16).

Jesus did not realize and teach the mysterious relationship between sin and sickness merely because He was an astute observer of human psychology. Rather, He knew the hearts of men. He knew the mind of His Heavenly Father who created men to live in truth and total submission to God. That is why He preached constantly the conversion of the heart back to God. Then the new creation would be experienced, the Kingdom of God, of love, peace and joy (Ga 5:22) would already be experienced.

JESUS COMMISSIONS OTHERS TO HEAL

The Kingdom of God was to be effected through the teaching and healing power that Jesus gave to His disciples and followers. He promised that they would do even greater things because He and the Father would abide with their

Holy Spirit (Jn 14:12-13). Without Jesus they could do nothing (Jn 15:4). But if they remained in Him they could effectively do great things.

> If you remain in me
> and my words remain in you,
> you may ask what you will
> and you shall get it (Jn 15:7).

Before Jesus ascended into Heaven, He commissioned His disciples to go to all parts of the earth preaching His doctrine of salvation and the belief in Him through Baptism and healing all diseases.

> Go out to the whole world; proclaim the Good News to all creation. He who believes and is baptized will be saved; he who does not believe will be condemned. These are the signs that will be associated with believers: in my name they will cast out devils; they will have the gift of tongues; they will pick up snakes in their hands, and be unharmed should they drink deadly poison; they will lay their hands on the sick, who will recover (Mk 16:16-18).

The *Acts of the Apostles* is a continuous account of what the Holy Spirit, sent upon the followers of Jesus, effected by ways of healings. Peter had only to walk among the beds and couches on which lay the sick in the streets of Jerusalem and his shadow, falling upon them, was enough that "all of them were cured" (Ac 5:16).

The true followers of Jesus down through the ages have accepted in faith His commission to go forth and in His saving name to pray the prayer of faith and healings and miracles abounded. Only when the advice of St. James was not heeded and childlike faith in the power of His name and

His living presence where two or three would gather in His name wavered did the Church fail to see the healings that were so common in the early Church.

> But he must ask with faith, and no trace of doubt, because a person who has doubts is like the waves thrown up in the sea when the wind drives. That sort of person, in two minds, wavering between going different ways, must not expect that the Lord will give him anything (Jm 1:6-8).

PSYCHIC HEALING

Down through the ages, from the Scribes and Pharisees of our Lord's time who claimed that He healed by Beelzebub's power, to Origen's adversary, Celsus, to the Rationalists like Renan, to moderns who claim Jesus had a highly developed E S P power or was a superb hypnotherapist, Jesus' power to heal has been explained away by certain "natural" ways.[1]

Perhaps by approaching the healing power of Jesus in a different manner, we can gain greater insight into the person of Jesus and His relationships with us. The Western mind, with its penchant to distinguish with clear and distinct Cartesian ideas, usually approaches the healings and miracles of Jesus with a decided dichotomy. We are anxious to prove that He performed healings and miracles that had to come from His "supernatural" power, proving in an apologetical manner that He was truly divine.

Others bring forth from studies of comparative religions or from the world of hypnosis and other psychic phenomena similar healings and miracles and claim therefore that Jesus was using a "natural" power found in all of us.

Jesus Heals

The Incarnation is God's revelation in Christ Jesus that God is not only present in matter, but He is dynamically working at all times, in all of nature, in a very "natural" way to bring all things into a fullness by the power of His Word.[2] Jesus was in touch with God's uncreated energies in a way that no other human being ever has been. If God created man's psyche in such a way that the unconscious, receiving a suggestion from an outside authority, can unleash great energies effecting healings and miraculous actions normally not performed by man on a conscious level, is it less of God's power in Jesus if He works with man's nature?

Jesus used matter. He made a paste of spittle and clay and laid it on the blind man's eyes and told him to bathe his eyes in the Pool of Siloam (Jn 9: 6-7). He put spittle on the eyes of the blind man at Bethsaida and laid His hands on him and after two attempts He healed him (Mk 8:22-26). The woman with a hemorrhage touched Him and He felt a current of energy pass from Him to her. His Disciples were instructed by Him to anoint with oil and healings were effect (Mk 6:13).

Jesus often *gazed* intently upon a sick person in need of healing as did Peter and John in healing the cripple at the Gate Beautiful (Ac 3:4). Jesus often gave the suggestion, asking whether the sick wanted to be healed and whether they believed firmly that they would be healed. He called Lazarus back to life crying out "in a loud voice" (Jn 11:43). His casual technique was the human touch, but at times He cured people separated from Him by distance.

In all such techniques Jesus allows the sick the opportunity to become attentive to God's presence in Him. The ease with which Jesus touched all types of sick people and without complicated methods, healed them showed the early disciples and those who were open to His total healing presence that Jesus was God's sign of the coming of the Kingdom. Jesus healed, not so much by possessing a psychic energy that passed from Him into the sick persons, but rather by being the concrete expression of God's love for His sick children. Jesus, by His gaze, His touch, His whole gentle presence, opened the sick to the inner depths of God's presence within them. They yielded in faith to God's mysterious presence within Jesus that released God's loving, healing presence in them.

Jesus was telling them that on all levels the Heavenly Father was concerned and wanted them to be healthy, if they would yield to that inner divine power locked within them. The secret of Jesus' healing power lies in the fact that He perfectly imaged the Heavenly Father for each sick person who met Him. In the love that He poured out in each look and touch and word, He was calling the sick unto the healing love of God.

His Spirit of Love allows us to see and experience His presence as the Father's love, living within us and He calls us into healing unto abundant life. As we are healed on all levels: spirit, soul and body relationships, we are called out to be channels of God's healing love to each person we meet. It is God's love in us that heals us and allows others to be healed by our touch, our look, our word.

CHAPTER 7

JESUS: HOLY, HOLY, HOLY

Have you ever thought what Jesus would be like if He were to return in the flesh among us and walk again through the Bronx or Haight-Asbury? If He performed no other miracle than that of being totally available to each person, would we discern in Him someone outstanding? How would He manifest that He is God's holiness in human form?

No doubt our faulty, traditional ideas about what constitutes true Christian holiness would probably impede us from thinking He were holy, if He came among us and manifested the same holiness He showed to His fellow-Jews. The holiness of Jesus is God's holiness. But only the poor in spirit, the meek and gentle of heart are able to recognize that Jesus' greatness consisted in bringing to us an image of God's holiness and in giving us His *Holy* Spirit who alone makes us also holy as He is holy.

GOD IS HOLY

To describe God's holiness is to touch the "insideness" of God. God's power can be seen in His creative works of nature. But God's holiness is God in His perfection as good and beautiful and loving. It is, above all, God in the totality of His being, moving outwardly towards the other, towards man and angel, to offer Himself as gift.

In Holy Scripture, whenever God is described as holy, He is always close to man or angel, involved in a communicating of His loving nature so that His perfection may be shared in a union of love.

> For it is I, Yahweh, who am your God. You have been sanctified and have become holy because I am holy. . . . Yes, it is I, Yahweh, who have brought you out of Egypt to be your God: you, therefore, must be holy because I am holy (Lv 11:44-45).

Isaiah was swept up in vision before the throne of God and saw how the Seraphs covered their faces and feet and cried out constantly:

> 'Holy, holy, holy is Yahweh Sabaoth.
> His glory fills the whole earth.'
> The foundations of the threshold shook with the voice of the one who cried out,
> and the Temple was filled with smoke. I said:
> 'What a wretched state I am in! I am lost,
> for I am a man of unclean lips
> and I live among a people of unclean lips,
> and my eyes have looked at the King, Yahweh Sabaoth' (Is 6:3-5).

Moses also fell back before the holiness of Yahweh in the burning bush. For that was *holy* ground (Ex 3:4-6) because God who is holy made Himself present in that place. No human hand could touch the Ark of the Covenant because God's holy presence was in that place. His holiness was localized in the Inner Sanctum, in the Holy of Holies, for it was there Yahweh promised to enter into His special, loving communication with His people.

God creates, but He is more perfectly present to man when His holiness touches man to sanctify him. God's holy presence is God entering upon a self-giving that allows man to be a sharer, through love, in His very own nature. This has always been the end of man:

> . . . be holy in all you do, since it is the Holy One who has called you, and scripture says: Be holy, for I am holy (1 P 1:15-16).

God calls us to receive His holiness and to become holy as He is, to open ourselves to His outpouring love and gift of Himself for us and then to become outpoured gift in love of Him and neighbor. We are called to be saints, or holy people, sanctified by God's holiness (Rm 1:7; 1 Co 1:2). "We have been called by God to be holy, not to be immoral" (1 Th 4:7). God chose us from the beginning to be holy by the sanctifying power of the Holy Spirit (2 Th 2:13), "chose us in Christ to be *holy* and spotless, and to live through love in his presence, determining that we should become his adopted sons through Jesus Christ . . ." (Ep 1:4-5).

JESUS—HOLY

Jesus is holy. And we are called to be holy. But we have no way of experiencing the fullness of God's holiness except in Jesus Christ. His role is to teach us about God's holiness that forces Him to be a concerned Father in all details of our daily existence. But, more importantly, Jesus comes to act out God's holiness. Now we know the answer to the question: What is God's holiness like? It is like the holiness of Jesus.

The holiness of Jesus consisted first in His having been sanctified by the Holy Spirit. He was the gift of the Father through the Spirit. All that He had came to Him from the Father. He can do nothing of Himself but only from what He receives from His Father (Jn 5:19; 30; Jn 8:28). It is the Father who has sent Him into the world and consecrated Him, made Him holy in order to bring God's holiness to the world (Jn 10:36).

Yet Jesus also throughout His whole life, in cooperation with the Holy Spirit, had to strive to become holy. In the Last Supper, Jesus prays to His Father:

> As you sent me into the world,
> I have sent them into the world,
> and for their sake I consecrate myself,
> so that they too may be consecrated in truth (Jn 17:18).

He was driven into the desert by the Holy Spirit (Mk 1:12) and there He was tempted. He was tempted and was like us in all things save sin (Heb 4:15).

> Now you know that he appeared in order to abolish sin, and that in him there is no sin; anyone who lives in God does not sin . . . (1 Jn 3:5-6).

Jesus was sinless because He yielded to God's Spirit within Him and went against any urge toward independence.

JESUS TEMPTED

We see the early Christian believers describing in the Synoptic accounts of Jesus' temptations in the desert their belief that Jesus progressed in holiness by overcoming temptations (Mt 4:1-11; Mk 1:12-13; Lk 4:1-13). There have been many attempts by biblical exegetes to explain the desert temptations. At least, as we read the Synoptic accounts, we realize, as essential to the truth revealed, that He had to struggle within His heart to reach the state of loving, humble submission to His Father that eventually would mean His ignominious death on the Cross.

It is impossible to ponder how the Evangelists arrived at this reconstruction of what clearly seems to bear the imprint of an actual experience lived through by Jesus, even though the struggle may not have been an incident that happened only once as narrated. Jesus would grow in holiness as He fought the Prince of Darkness for dominance both in His own life and in the lives of those He healed from demonic possession. His struggle would end only on the Cross when He would be lifted up and His adversary then definitively thrown down from his throne and stripped of his power.

The holiness of Jesus is seen not only as the presence of the Father's Spirit in the Son of Man giving Him strength to unmask and defeat the Devil but also as a growing process which brings holiness to Jesus as Jesus confronts the Evil One and conquers over him.

The three temptations highlight Jesus' total attachment to His Father. Jesus is given temptations much as Eve, the feminine side of man, in the Garden, to take the initiative in His hands in an aggressiveness that would deny God's sovereignty over Him. He would not yield to feed Himself by anything but by God's word. Power and glory over humble worship to God were rejected by Jesus' quotation from Deuteronomy 6:13: "You must worship the Lord your God, and serve him alone" (Lk 4:8). Finally

Jesus claims His divine origin, not by presuming on God's power to protect Him, but by an inner poverty of spirit that puts His whole dependence upon God's goodness. "You must not put the Lord your God to the test" (Lk 4:12).

TEMPTED BY GOD

The Gospels present the peak of Jesus' holiness as an *exodus* experience. He was tempted in His growth in holiness to hold on to His own life rather than to surrender His life on behalf of sinful mankind. Imaging the Father's holiness in His own human development, Jesus grew in each event as He sought to do, not His own, but His father's will. "Here I am! I am coming to obey your will" (Heb 10:9). Jesus saw certain ways of acting as coming under His Father's commands and these He freely accepted to accomplish, even when it meant His death on the Cross (Lk 22:42).

His holiness prompted Jesus to a joyful response to do all that His human consciousness revealed to Him as falling within the area of the Father's wish or even, more sensitively, what would please His Father more. He could say that His holiness drove Him always to "do what pleases him" (Jn 8:29). It is the terrifying abandonment by His loving Father on the Cross that becomes for Jesus His last temptation and the greatest (Mk 15:34). Unlike the surrender of Himself in the desert and the Garden of Gethsemane where He is consoled by the Father's presence of an angel, on the Cross darkness yields to more darkness.

Jesus who had tasted the joys of loving His Father, now tastes only a seeming hostility of the Father towards Him. He who was without sin, "for our sake God made the sinless one into sin" (2 Co 5:21). Here do the love and holiness of

Jesus for His Father shine forth in darkness. *Brightness* becomes *darkness,* holiness becomes sin for us. The Father did not spare His Son but gave Him up for all of us (Rm 8:32; see also Ac 2:23).

His whole earthly life was focused on being about His Father's business (Lk 2:50). Yet in the greatest temptation on the Cross, the final thrust towards fullness of holiness, Jesus feels that, although He is choosing only the Father's will, the Father does not seem to be present, interested or concerned at all with Him. More, Jesus seems to be rejected cruelly by His Father. Yet He remains faithful. Holiness ultimately is total surrender to God, even if God seemingly rejects the gift. In this, His greatest temptation, Jesus is tempted to doubt, in the absence of the Father's loving approval, His own identity. Perhaps the crowd is right after all. "If you are God's son, come down from the cross!" (Mt 27:40).

In spite of His temptations, Jesus pushes to new depths of holiness and loving surrender as He cries out, "Father!" He still gives Himself as gift even though the Father does not seem present to receive it.

In that struggle with His Father, Jesus attains, in His human expression, the holiness of God. This is the victory of His holiness and it is the crowning in human language of the Trinity's holiness, of self-giving to mankind unto death and complete abandonment.

Jesus' true holiness would come from humiliation unto exaltation, as St. Paul so powerfully presents:

> . . . he was humbler yet,
> even to accepting death,
> death on a cross.
> But God raised him high

and gave him the name
which is above all other names
so that all beings
in the heavens, on earth and in the underworld,
should bend the knee at the name of Jesus
and that every tongue should acclaim
Jesus Christ as Lord,
to the glory of God the Father (Ph 2:8-11).

HOLY THROUGH GOD'S SPIRIT

If Jesus, by the Holy Spirit, is glorified by the Father and is able to bestow His sanctifying Spirit upon His believers in His final sufferings, it is no less also the Holy Spirit who effects the holiness of Jesus at each stage of His earlier development. An important episode that launches Jesus towards full holiness, under the guidance of the Holy Spirit is that of His baptism in the Jordan by St. John the Baptist. Jesus receives a vision as He comes out of the water, seeing the Spirit as a gentle dove and hearing His Father declare from on high: "You are my Son, the Beloved, my favour rests on you" (Mk 1:11).

The heavens opened and Jesus is made aware in His human consciousness that He is hearing His heavenly Father and seeing the Holy Spirit come upon Him as the Father's gift.[1] Deep down the human Jesus is swept up into an ecstatic oneness with the Father. Like the water that falls down over His human body, so the love of the Father for Him as His beloved Son cascades over Him and covers Him with His glory. Heaven and earth had been closed by man's first sin in the Garden. Now God's communicating presence has passed through the barrier of sin and Jesus, God's holiness, stands within the human family. *Brightness* and *darkness* are brought together in Jesus.

And it is the Holy Spirit, the personalized, activating love of the Father towards His Son and of His Son toward His Father who is present, gently reconciling the darkness with the soft breaking of the dawn of a new age.

> In the evening, the dove came back to him and there it was with a new olive branch in its beak (Gn 8:11).

The Spirit brings Jesus, not in this one moment of His baptism, but in every moment of His conscious, human existence to a greater joyful and peaceful assurance that the Father loves Him. The Spirit gives Jesus the determination to be perfect as the Heavenly Father is perfect" (Mt 5:48) and the loving power to fulfill in all events that desire.

JESUS HUMAN

The presence and sanctifying action of the Holy Spirit in the life of Jesus begins with Jesus in His materiality. If St. Paul could appeal to the Corinthians' inner dignity because their bodies were holy: "Your body, you know, is the temple of the Holy Spirit" (1 Co 6:19), how much more was this a living experience of Jesus in His body? Jesus not only found the Father working in nature all about Him, in the fields, the sea, the sky, the changes of the seasons, the variety of plant and animal life, but also He continually discovered the Father in His own body, indwelling and working.

St. Irenaeus of the 2nd century could say that the glory of God was a man living fully. Jesus was the most free human being that ever existed because the Spirit in Him allowed Him to find the Father, gifting Him with himself in so many new and surprising ways. Seeing His Father in the materiality of His body as well as that of the world around Him, Jesus enjoyed a serenity and contentment in being *there* with the Father. Sin sets up a physical, psychical and spiritual *nervousness* in us because we fail to see the loving presence of God in those relationships. We tend to exploit them, as we see in our abuses of our basic appetites for food, drink, sex, material and intellectual possessions, honors and, in a word, pride of life.

The Spirit in Jesus allowed Him to grow "in wisdom, in stature, and in favour with God and men" (Lk 2:52). All anxiety was removed from His openness to meet His loving Father in each fresh moment. The situation was not objectivized as either holy or profane for Jesus. But from the inner presence of the Spirit, He moved freely through life's events and circumstances to respond fully according to the Father's mind. His life, made up of each moment and His free choices within that moment, brought Him into a growing experience that in all things He was the Word, one with the Mind of the Father. Free from sin and self-seeking, Jesus was free to be loved infinitely by His Father and to strive to respond joyfully in a return of that love.

Whether Jesus was lying on a slope outside of Nazareth watching the fleecy clouds pass by in ever-changing creations of beauty or having His feet washed by a prostitute, He found His Father's loving presence and praised Him with joyful surrender. Above all, Jesus was free to love His body as a work and gift of His Father and to use it to glorify Him.

Jesus was free to be most human. Whether He was eating and drinking at a wedding feast or talking patiently with the Samaritan adulteress at the well of Jacob, He could enter fully into that given situation. With joyful exuberance He could embrace all creatures and use them properly according to His Father's mind. Especially was Jesus human in His love for the special gifts of intimate friends His Father gave Him. He praised God for the gifts of His Disciples whom He ardently loved. He could praise God in the gentle love He had for His Mother Mary, Joseph, Mary and Martha, Mary Magdalene and the many other women who followed Him and served His needs.

Yet the freedom brought to Him by God's Spirit gave Him an inner austerity in all of His human relationships. His mother, disciples, friends were not His ultimate concern. He did not merely use them as instruments to glorify the Father but they were *diaphanous* points of finding the Father in the human context and to return love to Him by serving each human person encountered.

JESUS POOR

We cannot understand Jesus in His personal poverty and His preference for the physically, psychically, and spiritually poor persons whom He met and ministered His healing to unless we can enter into the conscious relationship that Jesus, as the imaged Word of the Father, entered into. His basic experience of God's love for mankind was that from man's side there reigned absolute poverty. Man is most radically and ontologically non-entity except for God's outpoured love in unselfish creation. God is absolute love (*agape*) because He is perfectly holy and self-giving.

As Jesus experienced, through the Spirit, the riches of God poured out, first into His humanity, He lived "poverty." Such poverty becomes a humble recognition of God's sovereignty and free gift of His love. It is a permanent attitude of mind that Jesus assumes towards Himself, His Father, and each person He meets. It is poverty that can be called humility. Jesus was nothing; the Father was all. He is meek and humble of heart (Mt 11:29). Jesus surrendered Himself to do whatever the Father wished Him to do, even unto death.

This doctrine was basic to His teaching because it was basic to His life. He lived poorly only because He lived by the inner richness of His Father's continued gift of Himself to Him. Jesus was born poor. He lived poor as a carpenter in a small village and as an itinerant preacher dependent on the good will offerings of others for food and shelter. He was not destitute or heroic in His poverty. He had wealthy friends and could enjoy the gifts offered to Him. But He was absolutely poor because no *thing* possessed Him. He was possessed only by His Father and so He used things only as an external expression of that inner emptiness before the Allness of His Father.[2]

As He lived, so He taught others. Those actually living poorly were more open to receive God as sovereign than the rich and secure. He lived close to poverty and human miseries on the physical and spiritual levels. Yet He sought to alleviate such poverty and misery in every form. There is no intrinsic value in doing without God's created gifts. There is value only in being free so as to be ready to accept God.

Ultimately Jesus shows His holiness in poverty by being detached and unpossessive from successful responses to His loving service. In His freedom to let people be free, to accept or reject Him and His message, Jesus most imaged the "holy poverty" of God Himself.

Remember how generous the Lord Jesus was: he was rich, but he became poor for your sake, to make you rich out of his poverty (2 Co 8:9).

JESUS SERVES

Jesus, poor, humble and loving, shows forth all of these characteristics of His holiness by His service towards others. We have already discussed in *Chapter Three* Jesus as Suffering Servant and in *Chapter Four* Jesus as Healer. He came to serve because that is love in action and He was acting out in human ways to love of God the Father. He who was one with God in glory did not hold unto that dignity, but He emptied Himself, taking on our humanity (Ph 2:6ff). He who was master washed the feet of His Disciples (JN 13:1-16).

He lived a life of entire self-denial and obedience to His Father. Thus He went forth with total availability, giving Himself to each person as He saw His Father doing. The Father's compassion for His children drove Jesus to act out that compassion. He never sought His own comfort when others needed Him. He burned with an inner fire to actualize the presence of the Father in the lives of all men that He met. "I have come to bring fire to the earth, and how I wish it were blazing already!" (Lk 12:49).

Jesus serves most by not only preaching about the Father's love but also by acting out this love. Throughout His whole public life, Jesus went about doing good, especially in the form of healing all types of sicknesses and diseases. He is never more the perfect image of the Heavenly Father than when He saw the multitudes fainting and being scattered abroad as sheep without a shepherd and He was moved with mercy and compassion (Mt 9:36).

Jesus shows us His holiness and the imaged holiness of His Father in His self-giving to each individual who had a need. He lives to remove from human lives any pain or suffering and replace it with exuberant, rich, happy health and fulfillment. His service is love enacted, even unto His death. No greater loving service does man or God have than to lay down his life for a friend (Jn 15:13).

JESUS PRAYS

The holiness of Jesus is shown also in His prayer life. The Gospels give us much teaching by Jesus on how we ought to pray. But they also give us nuanced pictures of Jesus at prayer. We see Jesus praying *alone* before His Father, even though He often does this before His Disciples. We can well imagine that He joined His fellow Jews in praying in the Temple and synagogue services, yet this fact is not described in the New Testament.

The Evangelists have grasped the intrinsic relation of Jesus' prayer and His holiness. From their descriptions of Jesus in prayerful communion with His Father we note that Jesus never prays as a means to run away from His life context or to seek the consolations of the Father. Nor is He totally absorbed in praying for whatever would make Him a more powerful *doer* of God's will.

The prayer of Jesus is tied intrinsically with the coming of God's Kingdom. At least as St. Luke presents Him, Jesus prays to His Father in what regards His mission, the fulfillment of His Father's plan. Jesus prays at His baptism (Lk 3:21), in the desert (Lk 5:16), before St. Peter's confession that He is the Son of the Living God (Lk 9:18), in a moment of joy filled by the Holy Spirit (Lk 10:21), before teaching His Disciples the Lord's Prayer (Lk 11:1), that Peter be strengthened (Lk 22:31), in the Garden of

Gethsemane (Lk 22:39-46) and on the Cross (Lk 23:34, 46).

Jesus usually prays in solitude (Mt 14:22) away from even His Disciples, deeply immersed for long periods, even all night (Mk 1:35; Lk 6:12). He seeks the face of His Father in praise and thanksgiving, in petitions that follow from His desire that God's Kingdom come. In prayer, Jesus touches the holiness of the Father and is filled with a like holiness that lives to serve the Father.

Contact with God's holiness brought to Jesus' personal prayer and His teaching on prayer to His followers, an innovation not found in the formalized prayers of the Jews of His time; it was centered upon the great *Shema* (Dt 6:4-5) and the eighteen prayers of thanksgiving, the *Tephillas*. This is the child-like cry to His Heavenly Father in the intimate terms of the Aramaic *Abba* (which freely translated approximates "Daddy").

The Holy Spirit filled Him with this filial trust before the holiness of His Father and thus Jesus, from His constant experience of the Spirit, would teach others to pray to the Father in the Spirit with conviction that He would grant everything that would be unto their total happiness as the Father's children. The Father always grants the prayer addressed to Him that seeks to receive more of His love which, in Lk 11:9-13, means that the Father will send to such that pray an outpouring of His Love, the Holy Spirit. Childlike confidence and perseverance are the results of the Father's initial answering of all prayers by an infusion of His Holy Spirit.

THE PRIESTLY PRAYER OF JESUS

It is when Jesus reaches the end of His earthly mission and is about to die freely as victim offered freely by Himself, the High Priest, on the Cross that we see the depths of His holiness. St. John's Gospel records this priestly prayer, but we must not see it as a fixed prayer said at one time or in only one place. It reveals the heart of Jesus present at the Last Supper, establishing the new covenant in His blood, the end of His earthly ministry. It looks also to His agony and to the Cross. His love in filial obedience toward His Father shines throughout this prayer.

In this prayer Jesus prays for His Disciples, for their work in bringing about the Kingdom of God, for the Church that would be built up in faith through their preaching of His teaching. We have a beautiful summation of His teaching on the prayer of the "Our Father" and other teachings in the Gospels. In a word, it is Jesus turned completely toward His Father in heroic holiness on behalf of sinners to fulfill the will of His Father.

JESUS IS LOVE

Jesus is holy as His Heavenly Father is holy because, in a word, He is filled with the Father's love, the Holy Spirit. All other characteristics of His holiness are summarized in the one phrase: Jesus is love. The love of God conquers in Him at the peak of His filial obedience to the Father in dying on our behalf. He is holy by being one with God's holiness. Yet Jesus in His human consciousness grows in great holiness as He gives up His will in order lovingly to do His Father's. He becomes God's holy Word in His obedience unto death (Ph 2:8). As He became holy by learning obedience, so must we.

> Although he was Son, he learnt to obey through suffering; but having been made perfect, he became for all who obey him the source of eternal salvation and was acclaimed by God with the title of high priest of the order of Melchizedek (Heb 5:8-10).

CHAPTER 8

A NEW HEART

God had promised His people of the Old Testament that He would cleanse them with clean water and give them a new heart and a new spirit.

> I shall pour clean water over you and you will be cleansed;
> I shall cleanse you of all your defilement and all your idols.
> I shall give you a new heart, and put a new spirit in you;
> I shall remove the heart of stone from your bodies
> and give you a heart of flesh instead (Ez 36:25-26).

The first man and woman conceived by God in the Garden of Eden are depicted as walking in His loving presence, communicating with God in the coolness of evening. "He put his own light in their hearts to show them the magnificence of his works . . . Their eyes saw his glorious majesty and their ears heard the glory of his voice" (Si 17:8, 11).

But man lost the presence of God in his heart. Instead of light, darkness covered his heart, his consciousness of his identity in relationship to God. He had been created with a hunger for God's beauty. He was made "according to God's image and likeness" (Gn 1:26) and thus there is the awful searching in every person for his true identity in loving relationship to God's communicating presence, His Word made flesh, Jesus Christ. No matter how much darkness covers man's heart, he seeks frantically for a way out toward God's light. Modern man sits in his isolated corner, sick, disturbed, lonely, angry and shivering from fright. He has forgotten the language of communicating with God. Materialism has dried up his heart and strewn the arid desert with tinsel and baubles, leaving man like a discarded Christmas tree on a dump heap.

Yet God promises to cleanse him with clean water and give him a new heart. The Jewish people blessed their children with a prayer that was a cry for God's presence to come again among them.

> May Yahweh bless you and keep you.
> May Yahweh let his face shine on you and be gracious to you.
> May Yahweh uncover his face to you and bring you peace (Nb 6:24-26).

God's face would be uncovered as men looked into the face of Jesus. "To have seen me is to have seen the Father," Jesus said (Jn 14:9). The Messiah would be a shepherd who would feed his flock.

> He is like a shepherd feeding his flock,
> gathering lambs in his arms,
> holding them against his breast
> and leading to their rest the mother ewes (Is 40:11).

Jesus said, "I am the good shepherd; the good shepherd is one who lays down his life for his sheep" (Jn 10:11).

The Savior to come was likened to a fountain of

salvation that would pour out life-giving water. "And you will draw water joyfully from the springs of salvation" (Is 12:3).

And Jesus cried out in a loud voice:

> If any man is thirsty, let him come to me!
> Let the man come and drink who believes in me!
> As scripture says: From his breast shall flow fountains
>   of living water.
> He was speaking of the Spirit which those who believed in him
> were to receive; for there was no Spirit as yet,
> because Jesus had not yet been glorified (Jn 7:37-39).

FOOLISHNESS TO THE GREEKS

But when God spoke His Word in human form, His appearance was different from what the Jews were expecting. He came in no worldly power, but in the form of a weak baby. Instead of riches, He was born in a stable, wrapt in swaddling clothes and placed in a manger. He spent 30 years in hidden obscurity, poor, prayerful, engaged in the work of a carpenter, doing His Father's will and preparing Himself for "His hour." God was speaking no longer through His chosen prophets, "but in our own time, the last days, he has spoken to us through his Son, the Son that he has appointed to inherit everything and through whom he made everything there is" (Heb 1:1-2).

Now God is speaking to us in this person, Jesus Christ. Not only does He speak to our ears in the teachings of Jesus, but He speaks to our *eyes*. His Word is a visible Word to be seen and contemplated. This light, shining in our darkness, reflects as a perfect image the light of the Father's countenance (Col. 1:15). "In his body lives the fulness of divinity, and in him you too find your own fulfillment, in the one who is the head of every Sovereignty and Power" (Col 2:9).

God has now "pitched His tent" among us, a Voice, the Word of God, always present to us if we care to contemplate God's Speech. A new commandment of universal love is given to us "because the night is over and the real light is already shining" (1 Jn 2:8). Jesus has come to open us to a new age. He shows us the beauty of our Heavenly Father through His humility, poverty, gentleness, mercy, healing, zeal, joy and prayerfulness.

But He becomes God's Light, shining before us most brilliantly when He is dying on the Cross out of His infinite love for each of us. When the hill of Calvary was covered with darkness as of night and the Light of God's presence seemed totally extinguished, then the Light burst forth with the awful glory of God covering that mangled body of Jesus. He was stripped of all beauty and comeliness. He screamed out in His terrifying abandonment by His Father. Still there is more light to shine. Jesus has still more to give us, more love to show us, more of Himself to pour out for love of us in total emptying.

> When they came to Jesus, they found he was already dead, and so instead of breaking his legs one of the soldiers pierced his side with a lance; and immediately there came out blood and water. This is the evidence of one who saw it—trustworthy evidence and he knows he speaks the truth—and he gives it so that you may believe as well (Jn 19:33-35).

LOVE UNTO THE END

When Jesus gathered His friends, the Disciples, together for a last meal, He is described as one with great excitement in His heart; He has now reached a peak moment in His life. Everything from the cave of Bethlehem, the small home in Nazareth, the desert temptations, the previous few years of exhausting travels to preach to and heal the multitudes led to this moment.

> . . . and Jesus knew that the hour had come for him to pass from this world to the Father. He had always loved those who were his in the world, but now he showed how perfect his love was (Jn 13:1).

Periodically during His public life this flaming love in His heart to accomplish what His Father had sent Him to do would flare out in words of ardent longing. "I have come to bring fire to the earth and how I wish it were blazing already! There is a baptism I must still receive, and how great is my distress till it is over!" (Lk 12:49-50). His baptism would be of water and blood poured out from His loving heart, the heart of suffering God imaged in Jesus. When the spear would open His heart and there would pour forth the last drops of water and blood, then Jesus' work would be consummated. "It is accomplished" (Jn 19:30). What is? The end of the Incarnation. God in man has now finally spoken His definitive Word in Jesus Christ. St. John standing at the foot of the Cross has nothing to say. He invites us to "see" the Word being spoken clearly, telling us at that moment of God's infinite love for us. The horrendous folly of the sufferings of Christ is sheer nonsense except in terms of the logic of divine love! For the contemplative Christian, poor in spirit, the awful *kenosis* or self-emptying even to the last drop of blood and water has fullest meaning only in being an exact *image* of the heart of God the Father in His infinite, tender, self-sacrificing love for each individual.

Jesus' question can only receive an answer through the power of the Holy Spirit leading us into God's very own heart, flaming with love for His children: "Was it not ordained that the Christ should suffer and so enter into his glory?" (Lk 24:26). We as human beings would always have entertained some doubt as to the infinite love of the Father for us unless He who so loved us as to give us His only begotten Son (Jn 3:16), was being imaged perfectly in Jesus poured out unto the last drop of water and blood! In Jesus, "finished" on the cross, not only do we reach the *end* of HIs earthly life, but we reach the *end* of God's giving of Himself to us. For not even God can speak another word beyond His Word spoken in utter emptying unto death in Jesus. Beyond creative suffering unto death there is no other language in which both human and divine love can be adequately expressed.

Jesus moved about in Palestine imaging the compassion of His Father for the crowds who were like sheep without a shepherd. He cured the sick and maimed who believed He could heal them and thus He showed them the healing love of the Father. He consoled the afflicted; He preached the "Good News" that He had come to bring God's peace to all. How full of love are His parables of the lost sheep, the Good Samaritan, the Prodigal Son. He had a preference for the poor, the lowly, the sinners. He called Himself "their friend." He loved them with that tender love that a mother has for her children when they are sick. In a word, He loved them with the love of the Father for them. "As the Father has loved me, so I have loved you" (Jn 15:9).

THIS IS MY BODY

But it is especially in the Last Supper that Jesus pours out in a heartful confession to His friends the great love He has for them and for His Heavenly Father. He acts out in beautiful, symbolic gestures the love in His heart that would be acted out definitively in the piercing of His heart on the next day.

But now in that upper chamber, alone with His friends, Jesus opens His loving heart to them. It is a humble heart that wants to serve as a slave. Jesus bends down and washes the feet of Peter and John, Judas and the other Disciples. The heart of God never bent lower to touch His children than in that gesture of humble service.

> If I, then, the Lord and Master, have washed your feet, you should wash each other's feet (Jn 13:14-15).

It is more than an example Jesus is giving them. It is an image of God's divine power placed at the service of men. "My Father goes on working, and so do I" (Jn 5:17). This loving service in action is seen when Jesus takes bread into His hands, then the cup of wine and lays Himself out upon the table under the symbols of His death: the separate species of bread and wine. His liturgical symbolism looks to His death and offering of Himself even unto the last drop of blood on the Cross. But at this moment in the intimacy of a last meal with His friends, Jesus is giving Himself solemnly to death on our behalf, ratifying by this visible, external ritual act the whole meaning and basic choice of His earthly life. "Now has the Son of Man been glorified, and in him God has been glorified" (Jn 13:31).

We cannot imagine the depths of love and joy in the heart of Jesus who is able at this moment to give Himself totally to us and to remain ever represented in the Eucharist at the peak of self-giving love. What a flood of newly experienced love in the heart of Jesus for His Disciples and, through them, for us as He gives Himself, not merely to death for us but unto a sharing in His very being with the Father by giving us His body as food and His blood as drink. All of His other powerful miracles and healings have meaning in the light of this greatest power of communication whereby He gives Himself to us in the complete gift. He finds a way to remain among us, imaging always the sacrificing love of the Father unto the last drop of water and blood for us.

He establishes by that act of self-giving unto blood the New Covenant between God and mankind. In the Old Covenant Moses and the priests offered the blood sacrifices of animals. Jesus gives His blood for the remission of sins and the life of the world.

> He brings a new covenant, as the mediator, only so that the people who were called to an eternal inheritance may actually receive what was promised: his death took place to cancel the sins that infringed the earlier covenant. . . . And he does not have to offer himself again and again, like the high priest going into the sanctuary year after year with the blood that is not his own. . . . Instead of that, he has made his appearance once and for all, now at the end of the last age, to do away with sin by sacrificing himself. Since men only die once, and after that comes judgement, so Christ, too, offers himself only once to take the faults of many on himself, and when he appears a second time, it will not be

to deal with sin but to reward with salvation those who are waiting for him (Heb 9:15, 25-28).

In making the first Covenant, Yahweh had promised to be faithful to His people if they would faithfully observe the Torah. He also showed Himself the patient, tender spouse of Israel. Jesus renews this tender, spousal love of God for His people. The Eucharist is the banquet and Jesus is the Bridegroom. The Church, made up of the community of individual believers in Him, is the Bride. Paul says: "Husbands should love their wives just as Christ loved the Church and sacrificed himself for her to make her holy (Ep 5:25).

This is the marriage feast which Jesus' Father celebrates on His behalf in giving Him to us. Jesus is full of tender love and wishes to give Himself, "to lay down his life for his friends" (Jn 15:13). St. Symeon the new Theologian (+1022) writes of this mystical union: "This union is truly a marriage which takes place, ineffable and divine. God unites Himself with each one . . . and each becomes one with the Master."[1]

His blood is given under the appearance of wine that inebriates the Christians with His delirious love. The sacrifice of Himself is for the remission of sins. It is not a legalistic *quid pro quo* arrangement to satisfy the demands of divine justice. The blood of Jesus that remits our sins and heals us unto eternal life is to be a daily experience of the depths of God's love manifested for us by Jesus' complete self-giving. His ardent love, experienced in the Eucharist which is a re-living of the same dynamic, ever *now* love of Jesus, God-man, for us, touches us and takes away the condition of sin in our lives. Loved so madly by God, we need not resort to sinful actions, words and thoughts that are ego-centered and destructive of community oneness. We can, by the power of the Holy Spirit, who reveals to us within these symbols of food and drink, the presence of the loving Trinity, let go of our lives and live and love as God does.

I GO TO THE FATHER

If Jesus throughout His earthly existence lived in a loving surrender to His Heavenly Father, how much more at the Last Supper and in the agony in Gethsemane, was He turned in loving adoration to Him! The goal of His life is to make His Father our Father. Now He gathers with His Disciples before His death and His heart is turned intensely toward His Father. He will give us the Father when we "see" God's Word most powerfully gifting us with His identical love. "As the Father has loved me, so I have loved you" (Jn 15:9).

He faces the Father with a filial heart full of adoration. Overcome by His majesty and power but also by His tender love for His Son, Jesus is full of gratitude for all that the Father has done in His life and will do in the final hours of His earthly existence.

> I have glorified you on earth
> and finished the work that you gave me to do.
> ... I have made your name known
> to the men you took from the world to give me.
> ... I have known you,
> and these have known
> that you have sent me (Jn 17:4, 6, 25).

He pours out a heart full of love in petition to His Father on behalf of His beloved friends and followers. He

A New Heart

asks the Father to give them eternal life (Jn 17:2). He wishes to share His joy with them to the full (Jn 17:13). Jesus prays that the Father will consecrate them to His truth and that, through them, all who come to believe in Him may be one as He and the Father are one.

> Father,
> I want those you have given me
> to be with me where I am,
> so that they may always see the glory
> you have given me
> because you loved me
> before the foundation of the world (Jn 17:24).

TURNED TOWARD MEN

The heart of Jesus loved his chosen twelve. He saw them as individuals, John the Beloved Disciple, Peter, James, Andrew, Thomas, down the line and He loved each to the depths. But He also loved them as a part of Himself. They were to be the pillars of His Church. His love for all mankind would go forth throughout the whole world through the preaching of these men. His gift of Himself at this Last Supper and on the Cross the next day was for them and for many unto the remission of sins. "... this is my blood, the blood of the covenant, which is to be poured out for many for the forgiveness of sins" (Mt 26: 28).

He affirms that He freely will give up His life in order that people throughout the ages may be reconciled to His Father and have life everlasting. This is His moment of pure love for the world, caught forever in an eternal *now*. For love of us, He is willing to die.

Still His ardent love cannot escape His impending

death. His gift of self is not an heroic offer to those whom He loves, not knowing whether or how His oblation will be accepted. He is turned, in that Last Supper, toward the Cross. He anticipates what is to come. In His agony in Gethsemane at the conclusion of the meal, He sweats blood realizing the cost of His gift.

Heaviness, fright, sorrow, disgust, loathing for what is being asked of Him in suffering by His Father, come over Him. Fear, a new experience for Christ who had always been so masterful and courageous, now comes over His whole body, soul and spirit. He is really afraid! "My soul is sorrowful to the point of death" (Mt 26:38). The calm majesty, the look of sweetness and dignity are all gone as He lies on the ground trembling in fright.

> I am like water draining away,
> my bones are all disjointed,
> my heart is like wax,
> melting inside me (Ps 22:14).

St. Luke, always so sensitive to psychological details, describes the fear of Jesus in His agony in Gethsemane: "In his anguish he prayed even more earnestly and his sweat fell to the ground like great drops of blood" (Lk 22:44).

NOT MY WILL

So great was His agony yet still more great was His love for His Heavenly Father and for us. With His whole being desirous of running away from what the Father was asking of Him, Jesus struggles to new heights of human love as He prays:

A New Heart

> Father, if you are willing, take this cup away from me. Nevertheless, let your will be done, not mine (Lk 22:42).

In a similar struggle to love His Father with His whole heart, Jesus in the desert surrendered to His Father's holy will.

> Man does not live on bread alone
> but on every word that comes from the mouth of God.
>
> You must not put the Lord your God to the test.
>
> You must worship the Lord your God,
> and serve him alone (Mt 4: 4, 7, 10).

In that cup of suffering which Jesus would drink to the last dreg were the insults and buffets He received before Annas and Caiphas, the physical pains of the ignominious scourging and crowning with thorns, the fatigue, thirst and loss of blood in carrying His Cross through the winding streets of Jerusalem. Finally He is stripped naked and thrown brutally upon the Cross. Heavy nails are driven into His hands and feet and with a dull thud the Cross is dropped into the hole prepared for it. His body lurches forward and its weight almost pulls the body free from the nails, but then it settles back to a three hour agony of excruciating pain.

> And when I am lifted up from the earth,
> I shall draw all men to myself (Jn 12:32).

MY GOD, MY GOD

Our frequent contemplation of Jesus on the Cross through the aid of plastic crucifixes or by details offered us by a baroque type of pious preacher or spiritual writer has dimmed the awful starkness of that scene on Calvary and hence we have failed to grasp the extent of Jesus' love for us and for his Father. Jurgen Moltmann, in his classic: *The Crucified God,* captures a more realistic picture for us when he writes:

> Jesus clearly died in a different way. His death was not a "fine" death. The Synoptic Gospels agree that he was 'distressed greatly and troubled,' Mark 14:33, and that his soul was sorrowful even to death. He died 'with loud cries and tears,' according to the Epistle to the Hebrews 5, 7. According to Mark 15:37, he died with a loud, incoherent cry. Because, as the Christian tradition developed, this terrible cry of the dying Jesus was gradually weakened in the passion narratives and replaced by words of comfort and triumph, we can probably rely upon it as a kernel of historical truth. Jesus clearly died with every expression of the most profound horror. How can this be explained? . . . We can understand it only if we see his death, not against his relation to the Jews and the Romans, to the law and to political power, but in relation to His God and Father whose closeness and whose grace he himself had proclaimed. Here we come upon the theological dimension of his life and death. Mark 15:34 reproduces the cry of the dying Jesus in the words of Ps. 22,2: 'My God, why hast thou forsaken me?' This is certainly an interpretation of the church after Easter, and indeed Ps. 22 as a whole had a formative influence on Christian passion narratives. But it seems to be as near as possible to the historical reality of the death of Jesus.[2]

The many messianic prophecies that portray a suffering Messiah reveal to us new depths of the love of the dying Jesus. Heb 10: 5-7 presents Psalm 40: 6-8 of the Septuagint Version as the loving surrender of the Messiah to God. It was not sacrifices or holocausts that pleased God, but He fashioned a body for His Servant who responded joyfully: "God, here I am! I am coming to obey your will."

The Prophet Jeremiah describes the prince and ruler of God's people as one who would "risk his life by coming close" to Yahweh (Jr 30:21). Isaiah powerfully describes in poignant details the Suffering Servant:

> Without beauty, without majesty (we saw him),
> no looks to attract our eyes;
> a thing despised and rejected by men,
> a man of sorrows and familiar with suffering,
> a man to make people screen their faces;
> he was despised and we took no account of him.
> And yet ours were the sufferings he bore,
> ours the sorrows he carried.
> But we, we thought of him as someone punished,
> struck by God, and brought low.
> Yet he was pierced through for our faults,
> crushed for our sins.
> On him lies a punishment that brings up peace,
> and through his wounds we are healed (Is 53:2-5).

But it is in the death-hymn of the messianic Psalm 22 that the Spirit of God brings us to a new depth of Jesus' love for us. The Spirit reveals to us the infinite depths of the Father's love for us as we contemplate the Suffering Servant, Jesus. The first part is the cry of Jesus to His Father in the darkness of abandonment that came over His human consciousness. The sky darkened and the raucous soldiers stopped in their ribaldry and mocking jests. Earth, sky and air suddenly froze in a mute stare at the white figure hanging on the Cross. A cry pierced the darkened silence:

> My God, my God, why have you deserted me?
> How far from saving me, the words I groan!
> I call all day, my God, but you never answer,
> all night long I call and cannot rest (Ps 22:1-2).

"Eli . . . Eli . . ." At this moment the Father of Jesus who had always been a Light, bathing Him with His smiling love, now seems clouded in fierce darkness. How Jesus must have thrilled at His baptism and at the transfiguration to have heard those words of loving approval from His Father, "This is my Son, the Beloved; my favour rests on him" (Mt 3:17). But now it is as though the Father's wrath is poured out against Him. Jesus feels the quagmire of the world's sinful filth suck Him down and cover Him with darkness.

Jeremiah had predicted the anger of God and Jesus becomes the image of that storm.

> Now a storm of Yahweh breaks,
> a tempest whirls,
> it bursts over the head of the wicked;
> the anger of Yahweh will not turn aside
> until he has performed and carried out,
> the decision of his heart.
> You will understand this in the days to come (Jr 30:23-24).

As Jesus surrenders completely to His Father's will, soft rays of light move toward the darkness just as the first sign of dawn with its velvet touch dissolves the darkness. In Jesus' despairing abandonment, groping to look again upon the countenance of the Father He adored so profoundly, He experiences the paradox He had preached to others: "Happy those who mourn: they shall be comforted" (Mt 5:5).

> Do not stand aside, Yahweh.
> O my strength, come quickly to my help;
> ... Then I shall proclaim your name to my brothers,
> praise you in full assembly:
> you who fear Yahweh, praise him!
> Entire race of Jacob, glorify him!
> Entire race of Israel, revere him!
> For he has not despised
> or disdained the poor man in his poverty,
> has not hidden his face from him
> but has answered him when he called (Ps 22:19, 22-24).

JESUS THE ROCK

Because Jesus was obedient to His Father, even unto death, "God raised him high and gave him the name which is above all other names . . . so that every tongue shall acclaim Jesus Christ as Lord, to the glory of God the Father" (Ph 2:9, 11). Like a dying man who sees a light coming toward him to bring him into eternal life, so Jesus sees again the bright light of His Father's countenance. "It is accomplished," the Father smilingly says. Jesus repeats, "Yes, Father, it is accomplished." Jesus, the Father's *Bright Darkness,* experiences a joy too profound and ecstatic for His human heart to bear.

His hour has arrived. He is now the perfect image of the Father's love for mankind. Becoming God's communicating Word of love in the *kenosis* of total emptiness, Jesus is overcome with the Father's love. His Holy Spirit comes upon Him and inundates Him with His fruit of love, peace and joy (Ga 5:22).

The Spirit reveals to us that, as St. Paul writes, the Israelites in the desert drank from the spiritual rock that followed them as they went, "and that rock was Christ" (1 Co 10:4). Jesus' side is pierced by a soldier's spear and from the heart of Jesus, St. John the Beloved Disciple notes, there flowed forth water and blood. Not only does this detail reveal to us the *kenotic* love of Jesus and His Father for us, bought at a great price, but it is a revelation in symbol that now Jesus, dying, is glorified by being empowered by His Father to send us His Holy Spirit.

A whole school of exegesis stemming from Antiochene teachers in the Johannine tradition, such as Ignatius Martyr, Polycarp, Irenaeus, Hippolytus and John Chrysostom, interprets the saying of Jesus in such a way that from Jesus' breast (or heart) shall flow fountains of living water.[3]

The Spirit is the living waters that in Baptism come to us from the pierced heart of Jesus. Jesus is the Lamb that is slain (Rv 5:12). The Spirit purifies our hearts, the deepest layers of consciousness, by revealing the love of Jesus for us in the symbol of His pierced heart. Contemplating the depths of His love for us, we are cleansed of self-centeredness. We can continuously approach this sacred fountain, the rock that is Jesus Christ and be washed through the Spirit's revelation of God's love in the water and blood of Christ.

The Spirit gives us an exchange of hearts as foretold by Ezekiel (Ez 36: 26-29). Through the Spirit we can recognize Jesus as the Lamb of God who takes away our sins (Jn 1:29). We proclaim that Jesus is "the Lamb who is at the throne (who) will be their shepherd and will lead them to springs of living water" (Rv 7:17). The river of life, the

Spirit, rises from the throne of God and from the Lamb (Rv 22:1).

> The Spirit and the Bride say, 'Come.' Let everyone who listens, answer 'Come.' Then let all who are thirsty come: all who want it may have the water of life, and have it free (Rv 22:17).

It is certainly the Holy Spirit who has revealed to mystics down through the ages as they contemplated the pierced heart of God on the Cross, that from that side of Christ, the New Adam, we, the Church, the Spouse of Christ, the new Eve, are brought into life.[4] They had pondered Jesus whom the soldiers had pierced. They had reflected upon Paul's words:

> . . . as Christ loved the Church and sacrificed himself for her to make her holy. He made her clean by washing her in water with a form of words, so that when he took her to himself she would be glorious, with no speck or wrinkle or anything like that, but holy and faultless (Ep 5:25-26).

More importantly, they experienced daily, in prayer, what it meant to enter into the "heart" of Jesus Christ, into the depths of His conscious love for each of us and there be reborn of His Spirit.

A fitting close to this chapter that leads us from the great love of Jesus for us individuals to His love for the Church is St. John Chrysostom's comment on the wounded side of Christ:

> The lance of the soldier opened the side of Christ, and behold . . . from his wounded side Christ built the Church, as once the first mother, Eve, was formed from Adam.

> Hence Paul says: Of his flesh we are and of his bone. By that he means the wounded side of Jesus. As God took the rib out of Adam's side and from it formed the woman, so Christ gives us water and blood from his wounded side and forms from it the Church . . . there the slumber of Adam; here the death-sleep of Jesus.[5]

The Church is formed out of the womb of Christ's heart that is an image of the heart of the Father. Water and blood, two elements symbolic of the creative forces of the female, symbols of the life-giving power that Jesus, dying on the Cross, gives to His Bride, the Church, signs of the birth-giving waters of Baptism and the nourishing Body and Blood of Christ. Before such infinite love of God, made manifest in Christ Jesus, our response must be a similar return of love by the power of Jesus' Spirit in us.

> With God on our side who can be against us? Since God did not spare his own Son, but gave him up to benefit us all, we may be certain, after such a gift, that he will not refuse anything he can give . . . Christ Jesus not only died for us—he rose from the dead and there at God's right hand he stands and pleads for us. Nothing therefore can come between us and the love of Christ, even if we are troubled or worried, or being persecuted, or lacking food or clothes, or being threatened or even attacked . . . There are the trials through which we triumph, by the power of him who loved us (Rm 8:31-37).

CHAPTER 9

JESUS IN GLORY

A story is told in the U.S.S.R. that in the 1930's a government official came to a certain village to deliver a talk on atheism. After giving all his fine arguments against the existence of God, he asked triumphantly, "Are there any questions?" Out of the silence a man stood up, opened his mouth and sang, "Christos voskrese . . . !" He sang the *tropar* or *collect* prayer sung in the Russian Orthodox Church during the Easter season: "Christ is risen from the dead, trampling down death by death, and granting life to those in the tomb!"

Anyone who has participated in the Easter services in Byzantine Christian churches understands the radical difference of approach to the Risen Christ from that of Western Christians. With the church at midnight in complete darkness and the setting of Calvary still standing in the middle of the church banked with flowers, the priest walks through the church with a candle, the Gospel book and an icon of the Resurrection. Outside he knocks on the closed door and then sings with joyful triumph, "Christ is risen . . . " As he and all the people following him enter with lighted candles, they shout the refrain: "Christ is risen! He is truly risen!" One experiences the new victory of Christ over death. He finds it easier to believe also that the same "divinizing" process has already begun in his life and in those praying with him.

For Eastern Christians the icon of the Resurrection is not an objectivized picture of the historical Jesus coming out of the tomb, with the soldiers falling to the earth in terror. Jesus, with all the saints standing in the background, is seen pulling an aged man out of the bowels of the earth. Easter is joy in the new act of God who is *now* restoring man to new life in Him. A new creation, not only of the Risen Jesus, but of human beings sharing in His new life and of the whole cosmos transfigured by His glorious presence has begun.

Through liturgical and biblical revival, Western Christianity is recapturing the intimate connection between Good Friday and Easter, between Christ's sufferings and death and His entrance into His glorification. Both Roman Catholics and Protestants had been too absorbed for many centuries in an *atonement* theology that sprang chiefly from St. Anselm's speculations. When Jesus on the Cross died and paid back our debt to the Father, there was little importance assigned His resurrection in the history of man's redemption. In theology manuals it was like an afterthought: "Oh, yes, and then what happened to Jesus was that He rose from the dead and ascended to Heaven where He now sits in glory before He comes back to us again in judgment."

A NEW TIME

But the New Testament gives us a different vision of the resurrection. It cannot be separated from Jesus' sufferings and death. Nor can it be separated from our new history in a life in the Risen Christ. The early Christian believers rejoice in Christ's resurrection because of the saving power, not only of His death on the Cross, but also because of His new glorious life. St. Peter writes:

> Blessed be God the Father of our Lord Jesus Christ, who in his great mercy has given us a new birth as his sons, by raising Jesus Christ from the dead, so that we have a sure hope and the promise of an inheritance that can never be spoilt or soiled and never fade away, because it is being kept for you in the heavens (1 P 1:3-4).

God has brought Jesus back from the dead "to become the great Shepherd of the sheep by the blood that sealed an eternal covenant . . . " (Heb 13:20). Joy is everywhere evident in the New Testament because Jesus has gone forward into a completely new existence which He now makes possible to share with His followers. "I was dead and now I am to live forever and ever, and I hold the keys of death and of the underworld" (Rv 1:18).

The Synoptic Gospels preach three essential elements in Christ's work of redemption. He came to establish the Kingdom of Heaven through His sufferings and death and also through His resurrection (Mt 16:21; 17:22; 20:17; Lk 24:46; Mk 16:15). St. Luke carries these themes into the first chapter of *Acts* where Jesus is described as showing Himself and telling His followers about the Kingdom of God and His promise of the Holy Spirit who would effect the Kingdom in their lives (Ac 3:81).

The role of Christ's resurrection in our redemption is more clearly articulated by St. Paul. " . . . Jesus who was put to death for our sins and raised to life to *justify* us" (Rm 4:25). Jesus "died and was raised to life" (2 Co 5:15) for us that we might have eternal life. In St. Paul's classical text showing how Christ's resurrection is part of our salvation from sins, he writes, "and if Christ has not been raised, you are still in your sins" (1 Co 15:17).[1]

A HISTORY OF SALVATION

This knowledge of Jesus Risen is what St. Paul prays for as a gift from God beyond anything his reasoning powers could arrive at.

> All I want is to know Christ and the power of his resurrection and to share his sufferings by reproducing the pattern of his death. That is the way I can hope to take my place in the resurrection of the dead (Ph 3:10-11).

It cannot be studied solely from the account of Jesus' resurrection and His apparitions. For the New Testament is a witness to the resurrection and glorification of Jesus of Nazareth by men and women who met the historical Jesus in events that were rooted in a faith experience. Jesus risen was able to send them His vivifying Spirit Who could lead them into the *now* experience of Jesus raising them beyond sin and death into a share of His resurrection and eternal life.

Jurgen Moltmann furnishes us with an understanding of the new concept of history that Jesus' resurrection brings to believers. Oscar Cullmann had used the words *chronos* and *chairos* to contrast the interaction of horizontal, "chronological" time with salvific time of salvation. Moltmann shows how Jesus is inserted into human history through the resurrection by means of being a new creation, a new beginning, that shatters all historical categories. *Historisch* is for him the unredeemed past and present, our history that is doomed to death. *Geschichtlich* is the new historical reality of Christ's new resurrectional creation that allows us to live the eschatological future. It has happened once in secular history when Christ conquered death and now it is always happening, but not yet in its full manifestation.[2]

> The raising of Christ is then to be called 'historic' (*geschichtlich*), not because it took place *in* history to which other categories of some sort provide a key, but it is to be called historic because, by pointing the way to future events, it *makes* history in which we can and must live. It is historic, because it discloses an eschatological future.[3]

That the resurrection of Jesus happened sometime in history between Good Friday after He died and His Easter appearances to His followers is evident from Paul's appeal (1 Co 15:3-5) to eye-witnesses. It was that historical person that St. Peter points out to the Jews, Jesus the Nazarene who worked miracles and signs among them and whom they "took and had crucified by men outside the Law" (Ac 2:22-23).

But the actual happening of Jesus' resurrection was not witnessed to by anyone. Only those who were opened to the presence of Jesus were able, not only to "see" Him as risen, but were able to experience His glory and know that they were sharing in that same glory. Jesus could not be seen by those who did not believe in Him. He was not "observable" in human form any longer as He was before His death. Then He was still one with a sinful world. There was something of the world's darkness in Him that allowed anyone to see Him with their physical eyes. He had laid aside His glory in becoming one with the sinful world. But now, "God raised this man Jesus to life and all of us are witnesses to that" (Ac 2:32).

The followers of Jesus never yearn in a nostalgia for

seeing, hearing and touching Him as He was on this earth before His death. They had experienced an evolution in Jesus. He had progressed forward. Not only did the Father exalt Him in glory and place Him at His right hand, but Jesus was now present to His disciples in a new and more involving way. No longer is Jesus physically present to them as before in one limited place in Palestine. But the disciples of Jesus discover that He is in His glorification now declared the living, eternal presence of God's love for each human being in all times. Jesus is now Lord of the universe and God of all. In the witness of doubting St. Thomas, he moves from historical knowledge to eschatological faith as he falls down to adore Jesus glorified: "My Lord and my God!" (Jn 20:28).

A NEW PRESENCE

Jesus condescends to accommodate Himself to His disciples by taking upon Himself a form or various forms of physical presence to them so that with a material body He was able to be seen, to speak, eat, be touched by them and to carry the wounds of His passion. To meet Jesus as the new Creation, the disciples needed to make the step gradually from the historical Jesus to the risen Jesus. Thus those eye-witnesses had a direct and personal experience of a "bodied" Jesus. It was because they did, that successive generations of Christian believers, including ourselves in the 20th century, could be brought into a "faithful" experience of the existing Jesus in glory.

When Mary Magdalene met the risen Jesus in a physical form that she thought was that of the gardener, she recognized Jesus in His word, "Mary," spoken to her. The early Christian community, though, through a paraphrase of John the Evangelist, was saying: "Do not cling to me as you formerly knew and loved me . . . Go and find the brothers and there you will also discover me in the only way I wish to be present to you" (cf: Jn 20:17).

Again the message of the Church in the appearance of Jesus to the Apostle Thomas is:

> 'You believe because you can see me. Happy are those who have not seen and yet believe' (Jn 20:29).

St. Luke evolves this truth of Jesus present to the Christian community in a new way in the story of Jesus and the two disciples at Emmaus. The Evangelist wishes to teach the necessity of Christ's sufferings as a necessary part of His glorification. He argues by having Jesus as Word in Scripture explain Himself as found in the Messianic predictions in the Old Testament that clearly presented the Messiah's glory as part of His suffering servant role.[4] Christ's glory was the goal and purpose of His sufferings.

> 'You foolish men! So slow to believe the full message of the prophets! Was it not ordained that the Christ should suffer and so enter into his glory?' Then, starting with Moses and going through all the prophets, he explained to them the passages throughout the scriptures that were about himself (Lk 24:25-27).

But if we examine the details presented by Luke, we see a deeper teaching. Although Jesus is physically present to them, nevertheless their eyes were kept from recognizing Him because they were still judging not by faith within the context of the Word's presence and action to the community of God's people but by the physical side of the Word.

It was in the "breaking of the bread" that their eyes were opened to recognize Jesus present to them. Luke and the early Church are saying that there is a new presence of the risen Jesus that goes beyond His physical presence. The Word of God is present and recognized as such not by seeing Him but by hearing the Christian community that gathers together through Jesus' Spirit and that speaks that Word in continuity with God's revelation in Tradition both of the Old and New Covenant. There can be no contact with the glorious, risen Jesus except in His Body, the Church that in space and time now makes Him present to us.[5]

Not only is Jesus present in glory in the community's preaching of the Word but He is also freshly present in the Church's *doing*. St. Paul gives an early belief in the church's Eucharistic *re-presentation* of Jesus for the believers.

> For this is what I received from the Lord, and in turn passed on to you: that on the same night that he was betrayed, the Lord Jesus took some bread, and thanked God for it and broke it, and he said, 'This is my body, which is for you; do this as a memorial of me.' In the same way he took the cup after supper and said, 'This cup is the new covenant in my blood. Whenever you drink it, do this as a memorial of me.' Until the Lord comes, therefore, every time you eat this bread and drink this cup, you are proclaiming his death, and so anyone who eats the bread or drinks the cup of the Lord unworthily will be behaving unworthily towards the body and blood of the Lord. Everyone is to recollect himself before eating this bread and drinking this cup; because a person who eats and drinks without recognizing the Body is eating and drinking his own condemnation (1 Co 11: 23-29).

EXALTATION OF JESUS

We have seen how Jesus' victory over sin and death has had outstanding, almost unbelievable results for individual Christians, the Body-Church and for the whole world, that at least potentially had the power to move into His victorious light. The *good news* of Jesus' victory is that human beings are now capable of entering into His glorious, eternal life by the forgiveness of their sins and by the consequence of being reconciled with God through Jesus Christ, namely, even now to enter into immortality and a share of God's divine life. For St. Paul:

> And for anyone who is in Christ, there is a new creation; the old creation has gone, and now the new one is here. It is all God's work. It was God who reconciled us to himself through Christ and gave us the work of handing on this reconciliation. In other words, God in Christ was reconciling the world to himself, not holding men's faults against them, and he has entrusted to us the news that they are reconciled. So we are ambassadors for Christ; it is as though God were appealing through us, and the appeal that we make in Christ's name is: be reconciled to God. For our sake God made the sinless one into sin, so that in him we might become the goodness of God (2 Co 5:17-21).

Jesus in His humanity is the first fruits of the new creation (*kaine ktisis*), the new Adam, and He holds out to all of us a rebirth unto new life through His Holy Spirit. ". . . it was for no reason except his own compassion that he saved us, by means of the cleansing water of rebirth and by renewing us with the Holy Spirit which he has so generously poured over us through Jesus Christ our savior . . . to become heirs looking forward to inheriting eternal life" (Tt 3:5-7).[6] God has set us free from "the law of sin and death" (Rm 8:2) and placed us in eternal life as children of God, "coheirs with Christ, sharing his sufferings so as to share his glory" (Rm 8:17).

Jesus is in glory, exalted at the right hand of the Father; still He lives in us. He works in our lives and through us in the world precisely because He is exalted and is now in glory before the Father.

JESUS — OUR LORD

The New Testament affirms that by His resurrection Jesus is glorified and given the name that signifies the meaning of the name, namely, He is now the *Lord,* (*Kyrios* in Greek). This name, especially for St. Paul, who gives the glorified Jesus this title, is Paul's most common way of designating that after the resurrection Jesus is truly one with Yahweh. Jesus now in glory possesses a messianic transcendence, an exercise of royal sovereignty and dominion over the entire cosmos, and not merely over Christians.[7] We have already mentioned that St. Paul is thinking of this exaltation of Jesus by the Father because of His obedience unto death whereby He is given a name above all names (Yahweh)[8] and that is why every tongue in all cosmic levels of life, the whole cosmos, should proclaim Jesus Christ as Lord (Ph 2:9-11).

LORD OF THE UNIVERSE

It is especially in St. Paul's later captivity Epistles to the Ephesians and the Colossians that we are presented with Jesus Christ in glory as the Lord or *Pantocrator* of the Universe.[9] This Jesus Christ is not equivalent to St. John's pre-existent Logos who becomes flesh, but the Christ who both existed as the image of the invisible God from all eternity and who grew into the full imageness by dying in weakness and being exalted in glory. But Paul gives preference to Christ's evolution from obedient human person to exalted Son of God who in glory becomes the measure of all creatures. This is seen especially in St. Paul's Epistle to the Colossians:

> He is the image of the unseen God
> and the first-born of all creation,
> for in him were created
> all things in heaven and on earth:
> everything visible and everything invisible,
> Thrones, Dominations, Sovereignties, Powers—
> all things were created through him and for him.
> Before anything was created, he existed,
> and he holds all things in unity.
> Now the Church is his body,
> he is its head.
> As he is the Beginning,
> he was first to be born from the dead,
> so that he should be first in every way;
> because God wanted all perfection
> to be found in him
> and all things to be reconciled through him and for him,
> everything in heaven and everything on earth,
> when he made peace
> by his death on the cross (Col 1: 15-20).

JESUS—ETERNAL HIGH PRIEST

As we have seen, the Father has raised Jesus Christ, His Son, by the Holy Spirit, making the weakness of the flesh (Rm 1:3) now the power of God Himself. Jesus is the

Father's heir, possessing by His new risen state the infinite power of the Father because Jesus is totally penetrated by the Holy Spirit. By the Father's gift of "the power of an indestructible life" (Heb 7:16), Jesus fulfills the prophecy of Ps 110: 4: "You are a priest of the order of Melchizedek, and forever" (Heb 7:17).

This power to save is utterly certain, since he is living forever to intercede for all to come to God through him" (Heb 7:25). Jesus sits at the right of the throne of divine majesty in the heavens (Heb 8:1). His eternal priesthood comes not from an earthly lineage or from any earthly force, but of a heavenly designation, by the free declaration of the Heavenly Father. Jesus as priest is ordained to make atonement for our sins, to win "an eternal redemption for us" (Heb 9:12).

Jesus is now in His risen, glorified life with the Father. He is our mediator, making intercession on our behalf. He no longer offers a blood sacrifice of animals, for the Temple sacrifice has been done away with. This eternal sacrifice in this eternal now is Jesus who is always offering Himself to the Father on our behalf, as He did on Calvary. Jesus "offers himself only once to take the faults of many on himself" (Heb 9:28).

He has entered into the Holy of Holies and there offers Himself for us. We have access now to enter also into the sanctuary, an approach before the Father. We are constituted by Christ's eternal priesthood, through our Baptism, sharers in His priesthood.

> But you are a chosen race, a royal priesthood, a consecrated nation, a people set apart to sing the praises of God who called you out of darkness into his wonderful light. Once you were not a people at all and now you are the People of

God; once you were outside the mercy and now you have been given mercy (1 P 2:9-10).

JESUS INSERTED INTO MATTER

But Jesus in glory, interceding for us at the right hand of the Father, is not "up there," as many Christians may draw a picture of the heavenly Throne. The power of the Holy Spirit raising Jesus Christ to a new transcendence, one with the Father in majesty, glory and power, is a power that places Him risen "inside" our material world. Because the resurrection of Jesus makes Him transcendent, it also renders Him totally immanent to our present, material world.

Jesus' resurrection, therefore, must be viewed, not only as the cause of His glorification and exaltation in Heaven but also in His efficacious, efficient causality within us and the material cosmos. This aspect of Christ's glory is often ignored. We refer to the effect of Jesus' resurrection on us individually only as something that will happen at the end of the world when we, too, will share in His resurrection. We need also to see Jesus' resurrectional presence and His intercessory power as a dynamic force within the material universe. By His new and glorious life, Jesus is the new Adam and Lord of the universe, capable by His new life to lead us, and through us, the whole cosmos, to a share in glory.

This is effected by the presence of the risen Jesus sending us His Holy Spirit who imparts to us the very "uncreated energies" of God, making us children of God. Such energies influence even now our bodies since we are whole persons meeting the Spirit of Jesus through body, soul and spirit relationships.

And if the Spirit of him who raised Jesus from the dead is living in you, then he who raised Jesus from the dead will give life to your own mortal bodies through his Spirit living in you (Rm 8:11).

But tied intrinsically to our material bodies that are destined to a future redemption through a spiritual resurrection is the whole universe. Genesis 3:17 speaks of a universal curse of God upon the earth and upon all material creatures through man's turning away from God. Man loses his dominion over the non-human cosmos; chaos, the result of sin, holds the universe in bondage until that bondage is undone through the Spirit of Jesus Christ.

Christ's glory must be seen in His relationships with the whole material world. Jesus in glory is an active leaven inserted into the mass of creation to raise the whole created world into the fullness destined for it by the Father. The whole of creation is, like a mother in agony before giving birth, groaning and laboring in pain until now (Rm 8:22).

JESUS THE RECONCILER

In St. Paul's captivity letters to the Colossians and Ephesians, written while he was in a prison in Rome prior to his martyrdom, Jesus in glory is assigned the role of bringing the resisting world of sin back to His Father. Paul points out Christ's prior existence since all things in the heavens and on the earth have been made through Him. But then he goes on to show the active role of the risen Lord in reconciling all things:

> As he is the Beginning,
> he was first to be born from the dead,

> so that he should be first in every way;
> because God wanted all perfection
> to be found in him
> and all things to be reconciled through him and for him,
> everything in heaven and everything on earth,
> when he made peace
> by his death on the cross (Col 1: 18-20).

Jesus Christ risen exerts, therefore, a universal and absolute power and dominion over all creatures. ". . . now he has reconciled you by his death and in that mortal body. Now you are able to appear before him holy, pure and blameless—as long as you persevere and stand firm on the solid base of the faith" (Col 1: 22-23).

We human beings must yield ourselves to His reconciling power and, touched by the risen life of Jesus Christ living within us, we are to become also reconcilers of the whole world with Christ. This is beautifully brought out by Paul in his second epistle to the Corinthians:

> And for anyone who is in Christ, there is a new creation; the old creation has gone, and now the new one is here. It is all God's work of handing on this reconciliation. In other words, God in Christ was reconciling the world to himself, not holding men's faults against them, and he has entrusted to us the news that they are reconciled. So we are ambassadors for Christ; it is as though God were appealing through us, and the appeal that we make in Christ's name is: to be reconciled to God (2 Co 5: 17-20).

Paul uses the Greek word *anakephaloioomai* (Ep 1:9-10) to describe Christ's ultimate role in "recapitulating" all things by bringing them into the fullness of the Father's eternal decree. An essential part of Christ's glorification, begun in His personal resurrectional body, but effected continually through His living members, the baptized Christians of His Body, the Church, is the "reestablishing"[10] of the whole world's lost unity under His own headship.

Christ, at the time of His death and resurrection, in microcosm as it were, reestablished or reconciled humanity in Himself by destroying sin, death and the distorted element in the flesh. In the second parousia, of which we will speak more in the next chapter, He will also reestablish all things by spiritualizing it. He will bring all things completely under His dominion by bestowing the fullness of His divine life upon men for all eternity.

Yet, in a very true sense, this reestablishing of divine life in the individual Christian need not wait for the *parousia;* the process has already begun in Christians through Baptism and the increase of faith. We see Christ's own bodily death and resurrection as the perfect type of our own individual dying, by the power of His Spirit, to the "carnal" elements in order that we might be reestablished by Christ's grace into the new creation in Him.

It is only man, of all God's creatures on earth, who is capable, by reflecting in the depths of his consciousness, of finding the nexus between Christ risen and the rest of creation. J. Huby, the Pauline scholar, has well synthesized how Christ gathers up all things to give them their fullest meaning in Himself:

> In Him all has been created as in a supreme center of unity, harmony and cohesion, which gives to the world its sense, its value, and therefore its reality. Or, to use another metaphor, He is the focus, the "meeting point" as Lightfoot puts it, where all the fibres and generative energies of the

universe are organized and gathered together. Were someone to see the whole universe, past, present and future, in a single instantaneous glimpse, he would see all beings ontologically suspended from Christ, and completely unintelligible apart from Him.[11]

The new approach of theologians to the resurrection of Jesus, inspired by the biblical and liturgical renewal within the Church, is to view Jesus risen as God's life working within the human context of our daily lives and imparting to us already a share in His resurrection. Not only has God within the Trinity received in Jesus risen a part of our humanity but our humanity and the entire material world have been swept up forever into God's transforming power. The action of Jesus risen inside of our human world is the action of God, revealing God's life and also bestowing to us a new share in that life. Jesus is the one "who brings the dead to life and calls into being what does not exist" (Rm 4:17). He was "raised to life to justify us" (Rm 4:25).

The resurrection of Jesus means for us His active presence as life-giving word, communicating God's very own life to all of us who open ourselves to receive of that presence. We stand in God's presence through the risen Lord Jesus (2 Co 4:13-14). Death is the absence of God's life and now has no hold over us (1 Co 15:54; Rm 6:9).

It remains now to see how Jesus risen effects the presence of the life-giving God within the community, which is the Body of Christ, the Church. Jesus is present and recognized as risen, He effects our own resurrection, within the contexts of His members in whom He lives by means of His Holy Spirit. It is through the presence of Jesus as Word preached and sacraments received, above all, as His love uniting all members into one Body that the risen

Jesus touches this world and raises it to a transfigured level of completion. Ultimately, the risen Jesus will be one with those who make up His Body, the Church. The Church is the result of the resurrection of Jesus, both now and in the *eschaton,* at the end of the ages. As the Church is now and will be, so Jesus is risen but is also a future promise whereby God will be always present to us in His Word, Jesus Christ and we will lovingly respond to His presence.

CHAPTER 10

JESUS SENDS THE HOLY SPIRIT

When Jesus sent the Holy Spirit to His Disciples, they experienced two actions of this Holy Spirit. The Spirit given them by Jesus filled them with power to preach Jesus Christ crucified and glorified, to perform signs and wonders, healings and miracles in order to spread the Kingdom of God among all who heard them. But the Spirit also performed a more hidden, and perhaps more important work, since it strengthened their preaching and witnessing. That was the working of the Holy Spirit in their hearts to effect a living transformation into Christ. Jesus promised that the Holy Spirit would reveal to His Disciples all that Jesus had ever said and done. The Disciples would understand all about Jesus in the circumstances of their daily apostolate.

Before the Sanhedrin they would be given what to say in their defence. "The Spirit of your Father will be speaking in you" (Mt 10:20). Not only were they told by Jesus that all power was being given to them to heal the sick and drive out demons from the possessed, but also, they like Peter and John at the Gate Beautiful, had to make the concrete connection through the Spirit that in the case of this cripple the power of Jesus was available and would heal him if Peter claimed it.

We have seen how Jesus was guided at all times by the Holy Spirit. He was driven into the desert and realized the supremacy of the Father over all other considerations by the

Spirit's presence and power. Jesus healed and preached by the Spirit. But only after He had died and was glorified was Jesus able to send the Spirit.

But who is this Spirit that Jesus promised to send to His followers? Was He different from Jesus? What can we gather from Holy Scripture about this mysterious Person of the Trinity?

THE SPIRIT IS A PRESENCE

When we look back with the light of Christ revealing to us the inner meaning of the Holy Spirit, on every page of the Old Testament we see the Holy Spirit as the loving presence of Yahweh. It is the creative force of God moving toward chaos and darkness and death and drawing the "void" into a sharing of God's being. In *Genesis* the Spirit is pictured as a great cosmic bird hovering over the earth, seeking to stir the cosmos out of its slumbering impotence to fullness of life. "The Spirit of the Lord brooded over the waters" (Gn 1:2).

In *Deuteronomy* the Spirit of God is depicted as a feminine presence, like a mother eagle, both protecting the weak and challenging the eaglets to greater life.

> Like an eagle watching its nest, hovering over its young, he spreads out his wings to hold him; he supports him on his pinions (Dt 32:11).

This eagle image was often used by the Israelites for they had frequently watched how the eagle would carry on its strong wings the eaglet and fly high up into the sky. At a certain moment it would dip from under the baby, leaving the eaglet alone in mid-air—to fly or to go crashing downward. The eagle would quickly fly under the plummeting eaglet if it was not strong enough to fly alone and hold the eaglet on its wings. Again and again the process was repeated until the eaglet finally flew and at last became an eagle!

The Spirit is God's *Ruah,* a mighty wind stirring a static world into whirlwind movement, a gentle breath of God imparting His very own life into man. "Then he breathed into his nostrils a breath of life and thus man became a living being" (Gn 2:7).

God's Spirit was a protective cloud by day over the Israelites and a pillar of fire by night, lighting their way in the desert. He was the transforming power that, in the anointing of the kings, like Saul and David and Solomon, challenged them into servants of God, teaching and ruling His people. He was the "seeing voice" of the Prophets Isaiah, Jeremiah and Ezekiel who foretold the messianic age.

Men were given new hearts by God's Spirit (Ezk 36:26). This Spirit would transform barrenness into fertile land. "Once more there will be poured on us the Spirit from above; then shall the wilderness be fertile land and fertile land become forest" (Is 32: 15).

God had prophesied that that living presence of His Spirit among His people would be poured out in a future age in great abundance:

> I will pour out my spirit on all mankind.
> Your sons and daughters shall prophesy,
> your old men shall dream dreams,
> and your young men see visions.
> Even on the slaves, men and women,
> will I pour out my spirit in those days (Jl 3:1-2).

The Spirit of God is, therefore, seen in the Old Testament as a presence of God, stirring men to a deeper relationship with Him. That presence is not far away, yet it cannot be seen. It can only be experienced—but only by those who search out that presence. "When you seek me you shall find me, when you seek me with all your heart" (Jr 29:13).

THE HOLY SPIRIT IN THE NEW TESTAMENT

Jesus is presented in Matthew's Gospel as the beginning of a new Genesis, a new Adam, the father of a messianic people. Abraham and David were the messianic forerunners who were types of a new nation more numerous than the sands of the seashore. Jesus comes as the completion, but even before Abraham was, He existed. He becomes man through the cooperation of Mary and the Holy Spirit.

> Joseph, son of David, do not be afraid to take Mary home as your wife, because she has conceived what is in her by the Holy Spirit (Mt 1:20).

The *Qahal*, the assembly of God's chosen people, begins with the Spirit breathing into Abraham and David and the forerunners of Christ a faith that would expect the prophecy of a new race to come from the Spirit and a virgin (Is 7:14).

In Luke's Gospel we are brought back in a parallelism with the *Genesis* account. The same loving presence of God, His Spirit, broods over virgin earth, now Mary the virgin. "The Holy Spirit will come upon you and the power of the Most High will cover you with its shadow" (Lk 1:35).

The Word of God becomes one with us within the womb of Mary through the activating presence of God's loving Spirit. Mary is full of grace and the Spirit inundates her, making her a fertile valley.

Elizabeth is brought by the Holy Spirit from sterility in her old age to a fertility. Her child, John the Baptist, leaps with joy in her womb (Lk 1:41).

Jesus begins His public ministry by receiving the Spirit who comes over Him in the shape of a dove as John baptizes Him in the Jordan. By the Spirit Jesus is driven into the desert, there to be pushed into conflict by temptations to surrender Himself in all circumstances of His life to seek only the will of His Father. Through the Spirit He preaches and works miracles. Before His death, Jesus described His real baptism that would come about by God's Spirit working in Him a love that would allow Him to suffer and die, giving His last drop of water and blood for His disciples.

> I have come to bring fire to the earth, and how I wish it were blazing already! There is a baptism I must still receive, and how great is my distress till it is over! (Lk 12:49-50).

Jesus would be baptized on the Cross in the Spirit of God's infinite love. His whole life was a movement under the guidance of the Spirit but it was leading up to His "hour" when the Spirit of God would lead Him into the darkness of His inner depths of consciousness and unconsciousness. Out of that darkness Jesus would emerge into light, His glorious resurrectional life, raised up to be the Son of His Father because by the Spirit, Jesus had accepted the infinite love of the Father for Him and had given back that love in the sacrifice of His life on our behalf. But before His death, Jesus could not give the Spirit to His people.

> On the last and greatest day of the festival, Jesus stood there and cried out: 'If any man is thirsty, let him come to me! As scripture says: From his breast shall flow fountains of living water. He was speaking of the Spirit which those who believed in Him were to receive; for there was no Spirit as yet because Jesus had not yet been glorified (Jn 7:37-39).

When Jesus was glorified "to the heights by God's right hand, he has received from the Father the Holy Spirit who was promised" (Ac 2:33). He could send the Spirit only after His death. But He had promised this Gift in detail to His Disciples before His death.

PROMISES OF THE HOLY SPIRIT

Jesus promised that He would ask the Father to send the Spirit of truth (Jn 14:15-29) to be with us, in the Church, in each Christian and to stay with us forever. The Church would be born by the Spirit coming upon the dying Jesus. His pierced heart would be the womb and His Church would be born by "water and blood" pouring forth from that heart of Jesus.

The Spirit would not only stay with the believers of Jesus but He would also teach them everything and would bring to their consciousness everything that Jesus had said and done.

> ... but the Advocate, the Holy Spirit,
> whom the Father will send in my name,
> will teach you everything
> and remind you of all I have said to you (Jn 14:25-27).

The Spirit will teach Christians about Jesus and will empower them to become witnesses of Jesus, just as the Spirit witnesses to Him (Jn 15:26). That same Spirit will unfold, unconceal the plan of salvation to the believers in Jesus and give them true judgment according to Christ's plan. The world's sin is disbelief. The Spirit will expose that and will lead the followers of Jesus into the complete truth (Jn 16:7-15).

It was therefore important that Jesus leave them, that is, that He not remain always in that form of human existence and communication with the Disciples, because the Spirit would effect a new form of existing. Jesus would be freed from space and time. He would be able to come and dwell with the Father and His Gift, the Spirit, within the very hearts of his followers (Jn 14:23). And so, after Jesus' resurrection, part of his glorification was to send a new baptism of the Holy Spirit upon His disciples. "John baptized with water but you, not many days from now, will be baptized with the Holy Spirit" (Ac 1:5). ". . . you will receive power when the Holy Spirit comes on you, and then you will be my witnesses not only in Jerusalem but throughout Judaea and Samaria, and indeed to the ends of the earth" (Ac 1:8).

PENTECOST—THE COMING OF THE SPIRIT

That first group of followers of Jesus was made up of men and women who were not considered great according to the standards of the world. Some of them like Peter had even denied Christ; most of them had forsaken Him before the scandal of a humiliated leader who was crucified on a cross as a criminal. They gathered in the Upper Chamber with Mary, the mother of Jesus, and prayed expectantly for they knew they were in great, urgent need for something to happen in their lives if they were to live up to the promises and commands of Jesus. Again Luke, the writer of *Acts* which could be called the Gospel of the Holy Spirit as it describes the transforming power of the Spirit in that beginning Church, parallels the account of *Genesis* and the new birth, the conception of Jesus, with his account of Pentecost. The same Spirit comes down upon all in that room. It is the birth of the Church, conceived again by the overshadowing of the Holy Spirit. They receive the Spirit of the resurrected Jesus. His coming is described as a powerful wind, the same *Ruah* of the Old Testament.

> When Pentecost day came round, they had all met in one room, when suddenly they heard what sounded like a powerful wind from heaven, the noise of which filled the entire house in which they were sitting; and something appeared to them that seemed like tongues of fire; these separated and came to rest on the head of each of them. They were all filled with the Holy Spirit, and began to speak foreign languages as the Spirit gave them the gift of speech (Ac 2:1-4).

Filled with the Spirit, they went forth to witness to this inner transformation by preaching and witnessing to the risen Jesus and performing signs and miracles. Peter preached to the astonished Jews that "what you see and hear is the outpouring of that Spirit" (Ac 2:33). The Apostles spoke in a universal language of love, symbolizing and anticipating the Apostles' worldwide mission. The unity lost at Babel, a myth of the disharmony and dissension introduced into the lives of men through self-centeredness, was restored. Everyone hearing them understood the Apostles preaching as if in their own language.

In that descent of the Spirit, Peter, the leader of the eleven, changed into a new personality. He had been a fearful person a few weeks before, denying his Master and running away from the cross of Jesus. As Peter witnessed to Jesus of Nazareth whom they, his listeners, had put to death, the Spirit revealed to him that Jesus had been raised up to be Lord and the Christ, the anointed Messiah, the long-awaited King, sent to restore the House of Israel. What must be noticed here is that Peter leads his listeners beyond the external, phenomenal signs. He seeks to lead his hearers to an interior experience, a desire to receive the same indwelling Spirit to possess their hearts, to purify, regenerate and transform them. Far from telling them to do something bizarre in order to obtain similar, psychological effects as the Apostles demonstrated, Peter insisted on an interior conversion.

> Hearing this, they were cut to the heart and said to Peter and the apostles, 'What must we do, brothers?' 'You must repent,' Peter answered, 'and every one of you must be baptized in the name of Jesus Christ for the forgiveness of your sins, and you will receive the gift of the Holy Spirit' (Ac 2:37-38).

We need only read in the *Acts of the Apostles* and the epistles of St. Paul the workings of the Holy Spirit within that small first Christian community. The Spirit that the risen Jesus sends by asking His Father in glory is seen as the loving force of God Himself, divinizing all who were open to receive His Gift. This holiness given to man to transform him into an heir of God, a true child of God (Rm 8:15; Ga 4:6), is the very indwelling of God's Spirit taking possession of the Christian, penetrating his mind, his thoughts, his actions with the very life of God.

POWER IN THE CHURCH

We see the experience of Pentecost repeated in many different circumstances but with the same results. Peter and John pray to the Father to help the Christians proclaim the message of Jesus with all boldness, by stretching out their hand to heal and work miracles through the name of Jesus. Power comes upon them and they proclaim the word boldly. ". . . Lord, take note of their threats and help your servants to proclaim your message with all boldness, by stretching out your hand to heal and to work miracles and marvels through the name of your holy servant Jesus. As they prayed, the house where they were assembled rocked; they were all filled with the Holy Spirit and began to proclaim the word of God boldly" (Ac 4:29-31).

In problems that arose they consulted the Spirit within them and within the *koinonia* or Christian brotherhood. "It has been decided by the Holy Spirit and by ourselves . . ." (Ac 15:28). The Christians seek the mind of God through the Spirit's guidance in prayer and fasting and then ". . . the Holy Spirit said, 'I want Barnabas and Saul set apart for the work to which I have called them' (Ac 13:2). "We and the Holy Spirit" (Ac 5:32) becomes the continued experience within that early Church, the fruit of Jesus sending upon those who believe in Him the Holy Spirit. Stephen and Philip, deacons, are filled with the Spirit and preach and work miracles with great power. Converts from among, not only Jews, but also the Gentiles are brought into the Church by the Holy Spirit being given to them.

The beautiful story of the conversion of the Roman centurion, Cornelius, illustrates the working of the Spirit in a universal way among all men who are eager to receive a greater knowledge of the living God. Peter understood, as he ministered to Cornelius and his household, that "Jesus Christ is Lord of all men" (Ac 10:36). Cornelius, by his great longing for God, received the Holy Spirit and spoke in tongues, proclaiming the greatness of God even before he had received the baptism of water.

THE DIVINIZATION PROCESS

Although the *Acts* describe the powers of the Holy Spirit working in the Christian apostles as they proclaim that Jesus is Lord, it is only in Paul's writings that we have a theology of what the Spirit effects within the hearts of individual Christians.[1]

The Spirit brings about a new regeneration. Jesus had told Nicodemus of the necessity of being reborn of water and the Spirit (Jn 3:5-6). And Paul over and over describes the chief work of the Spirit as bringing us into a new life, a life in Jesus, which regenerates us into children of God.

> ... the Spirit of God has made his home in you. ... Though your body may be dead it is because of sin, but if Christ is in you then your spirit is life itself because you have been justified; and if the Spirit of him who raised Jesus from the dead is living in you, then he who raised Jesus from the dead is living in you, then he who raised Jesus from the dead will give life to your own mortal bodies through his Spirit living in you (Rm 8: 9-11).

Because that Spirit of Jesus is given to us by the love of God that abounds in us (Rm 5:5), we are made from slaves to be now children of God. "The Spirit himself and our spirit bear united witness that we are children of God. And if we are children we are heirs as well: heirs of God and coheirs with Christ, sharing his suffering so as to share his glory" (Rm 8:16-17; cf. also: Ga 4:6). We are thus able to share Jesus' very own life living within us because of His Spirit that He gives to us. The repercussions of such an ontological change in our nature, now becoming, as St. John says, God's children and that is what we are" (1 Jn 3:1) are endless as we strive to live according to this inner dignity. We are called out of darkness into the light of Jesus risen and therefore we must put aside the works of darkness.

Paul appeals to this inner dignity when he describes the physical body as really now the temple of God.

> Didn't you realize that you were God's temple and that the Spirit of God was living among you? If anybody should destroy the temple of God, God will destroy him, because the temple of God is sacred; and you are that temple (1 Co 3:16; cf. 1 Co 6:19).

Paul assigns to the Holy Spirit the character, initiative, and salvific action proper to a person. We become alive by the Spirit so we must always walk by the Spirit (Ga 5:16, 26). Christians are of the Spirit, *pneumatikoi*, spiritualized by the Spirit, because the primary function of the Spirit is recognized in the creation of this new life in Christ Jesus. The possession of the Spirit was not the totality or the fullness of Christian perfection, but the Spirit was given as the "first-fruits" (Rm 8:23) and the pledge or guarantee of its completion (2 Co 1:22; Ep 1:14). The phrases, "in the Spirit" and "in Christ," for St. Paul are complementary to each other. The Spirit is given in embryonic form in Christian Baptism. It is like a seed which germinates as Christians live according to this inner power of the Spirit revealing the mind of Christ so they will progress into a greater likeness to Jesus.

Thus Paul sees Christians caught within the dialectic of two forces: the power of evil and the Spirit of Jesus. They must live according to the Spirit of Jesus. This Spirit creates the new life of Christ within them. He also fosters and brings it to its fullness in the proportion that the Spirit becomes normative in guiding the Christians to make choices according to the mind of Christ. Ideally the life of a Christian is freed from an extrinsic law and is guided by that interior communication that he receives when he turns within and listens to the Spirit of Jesus. "If you are led by the Spirit, no law can touch you" (Ga 5:18).

The Christian knows with certainty by the evident fruit of the Spirit that accompanies his choices of each moment and these are:

> What the Spirit brings is very different: love, joy, peace, patience, kindness, goodness, trustfulness, gentleness and self-control. There can be no law against things like that, of course. You cannot belong to Christ Jesus unless you crucify all self-indulgent passions and desires. Since the Spirit is our life, let us be directed by the Spirit (Ga 5:22-25).

The Spirit guides the Christian to respond constantly to the living Word within him. He reveals to man God's will through the community or the Church. He allows him to participate in the Holy Eucharist, the perfect symbol and sign of effecting what it symbolizes, the union of the one Spirit of Christ in the many members with all members seeking the unity of knowledge and holiness of a formed, unified community: the Church. These are the works of the Holy Spirit in the individual Christian: to bring him to respond to the living Word within him, to respond to the unifying, loving force of the Spirit within the Church and to respond to the union with one another in the Eucharist.

This Spirit of Jesus reveals to the Christians how they are to do always all actions to please God, to lead "a life acceptable to him in all its aspects" (Col 1:10). But this cannot be done unless we are ready to live the dialectic between the cross and the resurrection, between putting to death our carnal desires and putting on the mind of Christ. The Spirit comes to help us in our weakness (Rm 8:26). He prays in us when we do not know how to pray. But above all, the Spirit fills us with the inner law of charity. It is by the Spirit's love infused into us that we can put to death the old carnal way of thinking and living according to the mind of Jesus. Through the love of God poured into our hearts we can be always patient and kind, never jealous, or boastful or conceited or rude or selfish. We need no more to take offense or be resentful. We will always be ready to excuse, to trust, to hope and to endure whatever comes. For love is the greatest gift of God, it is truly the Holy Spirit Himself operating freely within us (1 Co 13:4-13).

TRANSFORMATION INTO JESUS

By the Holy Spirit we are transformed into genuine children of God and we grow into that divine filiation by His infusion of greater faith, hope and love. We live an intimate relationship with Jesus so that His name is not only on our lips and in our hearts, but we are given the gift to contemplate ourselves living each moment in His risen life present within us.

> Now this Lord is the Spirit, and where the Spirit of the Lord is, there is freedom. And we, with our unveiled faces

reflecting like mirrors the brightness of the Lord, all grow brighter and brighter as we are turned into the image that we reflect; this is the work of the Lord who is Spirit (2 Co 3:18).

As the individual Christian experiences his life in Christ, that very same Spirit *urges* him outward, not only to discover Jesus in others but to labor incessantly to bring Jesus forth. He knows with St. Paul that the Spirit is the builder of the Christian community (Ep 4:4). God's love is not solely toward the individual. It is universal and embraces all mankind. Hence the test of the Spirit's true working within the life of a Christian is found in love and humble service towards his neighbor.

My brothers, you were called, as you know, to liberty; but be careful, or this liberty will provide an opening for self-indulgence. Serve one another, rather, in works of love, since the whole of the Law is summarized in a single command: Love your neighbor as yourself (Ga 5:13-14).

Jesus sends us the Spirit that we may become His Body, the Church, by the fruit of His Spirit: love and humble service toward the other. This is the life of Jesus and it is the sign that He truly lives in us. The risen Jesus is found now in His Church. And those Christians are the Church who let the Spirit of Jesus transform them inwardly so that they can, at all times, love and serve each other and the rest of mankind so that Jesus will be all in all.

CHAPTER 11

JESUS PRESENT IN HIS BODY: THE CHURCH

The Synoptic Gospels of Matthew, Mark and Luke present to us a Jesus as the first Apostles met Him. The changes in their attitudes towards Jesus are also recorded at the end of the Synoptic narratives. They earlier had met Him as all of us meet a new friend. They ate with Jesus. Many hours were spent day and night close to Him, listening to His preaching, watching Him healing, performing miracles of all sorts, re-acting to the Pharisees and Scribes, above all, to themselves as human persons. They saw Him tired; they watched Him sleep. They saw Him praying alone to His Heavenly Father and they wished to learn His secret. They thrilled when He fed the multitude and when He rode on a donkey from Mt. Olivet into Jerusalem and the crowds wanted to make Him their king. They did not understand what He meant when He said that the Son of Man would have to die and they themselves would have to deny themselves and take up their cross and follow Him. There were many things they liked about Jesus and His teaching. There were other dark areas that they did not understand.

Jesus patiently had told them that there were many other things He had to tell them, but they did not even understand all that He had already told them (Jn 16:12). He would, however, send them His Spirit to enlighten them.

Jesus Present In His Body, The Church

In each of the four Gospels we see a radical change cover over the Apostles after Jesus' resurrection. They saw Jesus and recognized Him as the same Master whom they loved for three years. But now their attitudes toward Him change. In St. John's account of the appearance of Jesus on the shore of Tiberias, we sense this change. There is an awe and reverence. "None of the disciples was bold enough to ask, 'Who are you?' they knew quite well it was the Lord" (Jn 21:12).

In his account of Jesus on the road to Emmaus, Luke conveys this change from a natural knowledge that the Apostles had of Jesus and His teaching to a new enlightenment as His gift. The eyes of the two disciples were not only closed to recognize Jesus present but they could not understand His presence in the messianic scriptures and all He had taught them (Lk 24:25-27). Their hearts burned within them as Jesus explained the scriptures to them.

Jesus spent His time after His resurrection instructing His Apostles. Great changes took place as they opened to receive deeper knowledge about Jesus and their own role in continuing not only His teaching but also His very risen presence in the world.

> Then he told them, 'This is what I meant when I said, while I was still with you, that everything written about me in the Law of Moses, in the Prophets and in the Psalms, has to be fulfilled.' He then opened their minds to understand the scriptures, and he said to them, 'So you see how it is written that the Christ would suffer and on the third day rise from the dead, and that, in his name, repentance for the forgiveness of sins would be preached to all the nations, beginning from Jerusalem. You are witnesses to this. And now I am sending down to you what the Father has

promised. Stay in the city then, until you are clothed with the power from on high' (Lk 24:44-49).

THE CHURCH IS BORN

When on Pentecost they received the outpouring of the Holy Spirit promised by Jesus, the Apostles changed radically. Externally they found themselves truly "clothed with the power from on high" as they preached mightily with keen understanding of the scriptures, as they saw the sick healed by their touches, as they saw others filled with the Holy Spirit by their prayers and imposition of hands.

But the deepest change was an interior one. They were consciously aware at all times that the Spirit of Jesus was within them guiding them. The greatest revelation was to experience a new-founded sense of brotherhood, one with each other. They had first glimpsed such a oneness at the Last Supper when Jesus had given them His Body and Blood as their food and drink. In that moment of intense communion with Jesus they had felt His torrential love flowing through each one, electrifying them out of their selfish pride into a new-founded loving oneness with each other. It was there in that first Eucharist that the Apostles felt the unity of the embryonic Body of Christ taking form for the first time.

St. John records Jesus' prayer for His followers that they would continue in that oneness, so intimate that He compared it to His union with His Father.

> Father, may they be one in us,
> as you are in me and I am in you,
> so that the world may believe it was you who sent me.
> I have given them the glory you gave to me,

that they may be one as we are one.
With me in them and you in me,
may they be so completely one
that the world will realize that it was you who sent me
and that I have loved them as much as you loved me (Jn 17:21-23).

Jesus compared this oneness between Himself and His followers to that found in the vine with its branches. The life-giving power flows from the Vine-Jesus through all the member-branches. As long as they abide in Him they will bring forth great fruit. But without Jesus they were like dry sticks of dead wood (Jn 15:1ff).

Christ died and went away, i.e. He gave up His earthly way of being with His followers only to acquire a new presence. "I will not leave you orphans; I will come back to you" (Jn 14:18). "I am going away, and shall return" (Jn 14: 28). By sending His Spirit into the hearts of His disciples Jesus makes them aware that He is now living within each member.

ON THE ROAD TO DAMASCUS

St. Paul as Saul, the militant persecutor of the first Christians, knew Jesus as one who had been put to death but who, His followers insisted in some strange way, had risen and was still living among them. As he journeyed to Damascus, Saul was converted to become Paul when Jesus spoke the words: "Saul, Saul, why are you persecuting me?" (Ac 9:4). He was told that he was persecuting Jesus when he persecuted His followers. Paul never forgot those words and his whole life as a Christian and ardent Apostle could be summarized as a steady progression in understanding more fully the meaning and implications of those words. He developed his ecclesiology from a theological anthropology that he so often (nearly 164 times) phrases simply as a new existence *in* or *with* Christ. Durrwell insists that the meaning of Paul is that a new man has come into a new form of existence. It is not that Jesus exerts simply an influence upon the Christian, but the latter enters into an ontological relation of oneness with Jesus, "by a change transforming him into 'one man, one body' (Ep 2:15-16)—into the bodily Christ."[1]

Paul would write:

> . . . and you are, all of you, sons of God through faith in Christ Jesus. All baptized in Christ, you have all clothed yourselves in Christ, and there are no more distinctions between Jew and Greek, slave and free, male and female, but all of you are one in Christ Jesus. Merely by belonging to Christ you are the posterity of Abraham, the heirs he was promised (Ga 3:26-29).

He could move easily, in his writings, between the levels where he found this new life in Christ in process of dynamic, progressive growth, either on the level of the individual or that of the Christian community. He does not strictly distinguish between the building up of the individual or the total community, the Church, since he viewed them as two points of view of the same reality: the life of the risen Jesus Christ, living both in the individual and in the united members of Christ's Body, the Church. He also was convinced that there was no true sanctity or God's life outside of the organism he called the Body of Christ. As the individual Christian grew in holiness by serving his neighbor, so the Church grew in holiness.

THE BODY OF CHRIST—THE CHURCH

Paul uses the Greek word, *ekklesia* (Church), about sixty times and with a variety of meanings. As his ecclesiology developed along with his understanding of Christ's relationships to His members and to the cosmos, so he gives different meanings to the concept of Church. Whether he was using it to refer to a specific assembly of Christian believers, e.g. in the churches of Asia (1 Co 16:19) or to the universal Church (1 Co 12:28), Paul sees it as a community, a *koinonia* or brotherhood, of Christian believers linked together by the bonds of faith, sacraments, especially Baptism which incorporates the members into the community and the Eucharist which symbolizes the union of the members with the physical Body-Christ and deepens that union. There was also the bond of obedience to the appointed bishops and presbyters empowered by Christ to teach His word with his very own authority.

A definite progression is seen in Paul's understanding of Christ's relationship with His members. Earlier Paul stressed the living Christ as the source of the common, supernatural life within the believing Christian. He then moved to a greater understanding of the Church as identified in some manner with the physical, resurrected Body-Person, Jesus Christ. In his major epistles the concept of the identity of the Body and Christ the Head is not fully developed.

> Just as each of our bodies has several parts and each part has a separate function, so all of us, in union with Christ, form one body, and as parts of it we belong to each other (Rm 12:4). Just as a human body, though it is made up of many parts, is a single unit because all these parts, though

many, make one body, so it is with Christ . . . Nor is the body to be identified with any one of its many parts. . . . Now you together are Christ's body; but each of you is a different part of it (1 Co 12:12-27).

In Paul's later epistles, especially to the Colossians and Ephesians, he clearly identifies the Christian people as the Body of Christ, one with Him. Christ loves this Body, the Church, cherishing and nourishing it. ". . . it is his body—and we are its living parts" (Ep 5:30). Christ is the head of this Body who nourishes and strengthens the whole Body with a divine growth (Col 2: 19). The whole body is dependent on Christ. Each part is brought into an harmonious knitting together through the energy that comes from Jesus Christ, the source of supply. The body grows and builds itself up through love (Ep 4: 16; cf.: Col 1:18, 24; Ep 1:22, 23; 4:15; 5:23). The Church is intimately related to the risen Body-Person, Jesus Christ who is "the ruler of everything, the head of the Church, which is his body, the fullness of him who fills the whole creation" (Ep 1:20-23).

A distinction in the ways Paul uses the Greek word *Soma,* Body, is perhaps in order. It fundamentally refers to the historical body of Jesus that the Apostles saw and touched. That Body was risen from the dead, the whole Body-Person, Jesus Christ living in His new resurrectional life. His Body is also given as food in the Eucharist. And then His Body refers to His Church, of which He is the Head and His Christian members are true parts of this Body. We can say that there is absolute identity between the historical and the risen Jesus Christ. The Body of Christ referring to the total Church with Christ as the Head cannot be ontologically identical with the historical or the risen

Jesus. There is, however, a partial identity since the very life that infuses the members, making them living parts of Christ's Body, is identical with the divine life of the physical Christ. Even though the Christians in Baptism and the Eucharist and through other means of receiving grace partake of the same divine life, they still remain themselves with their own personalities and life.

THE MYSTICAL BODY

Unfortunately the word *mystical* in the West has lost its original Greek sense. For many of us to call the Church the Mystical Body of Christ is to give to the Church a rather nebulous reality. It seems to imply that Christ is present to the members of His Body-Church by either a moral or an "ethereal" union. This lessens the full power of the Pauline doctrine of Christ's presence in His members through an ontological, real presence of the risen Jesus sharing His very life with His members.

Pierre Benoit, O.P. describes this union as a physical reality of a unique type with no other comparison known. The spiritual (pneumatic) body of the living, risen Christ (1 Co 15:44) is the bestower of the regenerated life of salvation to human beings. It is under the form of a physical (sacramental) union of the body of the Christian with the individual body of Christ. "Without a doubt this 'physical' reality is of a very special type, completely new which is that of the eschatological era begun while the old era still continues."[2]

The risen Savior lives within the Christian, releasing His Holy Spirit that the individual member may go out to the other actual or potential members of Christ's Body and by love let the Spirit bind them into a greater union. We perhaps might regret the nebulous implications of the term Mystical Body when applied to this very dynamic living relationship between Jesus and His members. Still the term has a legitimate theological development out of St. Paul's teaching that throughout the centuries presents to us an orthodox doctrine that avoids on the one hand a purely physical union with Christ and on the other a purely moral aggregate. The encyclical of Pope Piux XII, *Mystici Corporis,* is one of the finest teachings on the subject in modern times that brings together the best in Pauline exegesis.

Because Christ, therefore, in His risen, glorified life through His spiritualized "physical" body lives through grace in the members of His Body, the Church, this relationship between Christ and members admits of an ongoing growth process that will continue even into the life after death.

JESUS CHRIST—THE HEAD

Jesus is risen and lives within the Christian. He has already justified His members; they are saved. He called those he intended for this; those he called he justified, and with those he justified he shared his glory" (Rm 8:30). Paul even has us raised up with God who has given us "a place with him in heaven, in Christ Jesus" (Ep 2:6). Yet we members know from our own experience and that of the Church of Christ that we can still sin and we can still grow in greater union with Jesus. We share still a oneness with the darkness all about us. The awful tension of living in the glorious light of Jesus, sharing His resurrectional life within us by His indwelling, and of still living in darkness of sin in our members, within our minds and bodies, is a daily experience for us all. Paul could write powerfully that it is in hope for salvation that is still in process of being realized:

> . . . all of us who possess the first-fruits of the Spirit, we too groan inwardly as we wait for our bodies to be set free. For we must be content to hope that we shall be saved—our salvation is not in sight, we should not have to be hoping for it if it were—but, as I say, we must hope to be saved since we are not saved yet—it is something we must wait for with patience (Rm 8:23-25).

In Paul's later epistles to *Colossians* and *Ephesians* he reaches the well developed teaching of jesus as Head of the Body, the Church.[3]

Jesus has been appointed by His Father with complete authority over the Church. This is highlighted clearly in *Ephesians:*

> He has put all things under his feet and made him, as the ruler of everything, the head of the Church; which is his body, the fullness of him who fills the whole creation (Ep 1:22-23).

Jesus is the head but not solely in the sense of authority, such as a president of a corporation is the head. He is the Head of the Body not only by His authority that He imparts to His Church teachers and pastors, but He is the principle of life, the one who gives nourishment and sustenance so that the members can live *in* Him. ". . . Christ who is the head by whom the whole body is fitted and joined together, every joint adding its own strength" (Ep 4:16).

DIFFERENT PARTS IN THE BODY OF CHRIST

Jesus is present to His members by His filling activity. "Each one of us, however, has been given his own share of grace, given as Christ allotted it" (Ep 4:7). It is truly Jesus living in each member in a special way that is unique, quite different from the way He lives and operates in someone else. Paul brings this out in his description of the hierarchical divisions within the Body-Church. Jesus fills all the members with all graces (Ep 1:23) but He gives particular graces—He operates in specialized ways in individuals, all in order to build up the entire Body. These are charisms that the Spirit of Jesus effects for the good of the whole. This is clearly brought out in Paul's well known listing of charisms in *1 Corinthians:*

> There is a variety of gifts but always the same Spirit; there are all sorts of service to be done, but always to the same Lord; working in all sorts of different ways in different people, it is the same God who is working in all of them. The particular way in which the Spirit is given to each person is for a good purpose. One may have the gift of preaching with wisdom, given him by the same Spirit; and another the gift of faith given by the same Spirit; another again the gift of healing, through this one Spirit; one, the power of miracles; another, prophecy; another the gift of recognizing spirits; another the gift of tongues and another the ability to interpret them. All these are the work of one and the same Spirit, who distributes different gifts to different people just as he chooses (1 Co 12:4-11).

We can thrill at the goodness of God who pours out into us special gifts that we can knowingly exercise in the building up of the Body, the Church. But Paul also gives, as stated above, hierarchical divisions in order to bring the charisms into harmony and order, to build up truly the Body of Christ. A presence that we need to discover and live by in our modern age is the presence of Jesus in the authority that He has established to rule His Church with His very mind. The priestly, prophetic and royal authority of Jesus Christ is maintained by an hierarchical authority that brings the members into touch with the living Jesus in His Body. Paul shows the relationship between proper growth and unity in the building up of the Body-Church in his listing of hierarchical functions:

> And to some, his gift was that they should be apostles; to some, prophets; to some, evangelists; to some, pastors and teachers; so that the saints together make a unity in the work of service, building up the body of Christ. In this way we are all to come to unity in our faith and in our knowledge of the Son of God, until we become the perfect Man, fully mature with the fulness of Christ himself (Ep 4:11-13).

In our modern secularist society with distorted ideas about equality of man and democracy which allows license to reign in place of disciplined freedom, we have need to see the loving presence of Jesus as an authority on the horizontal plane of a divine-human Church. Perhaps nowhere else is the tension between light and darkness seen than in the areas of Christ's authority exercised by human instruments who can so easily fail to be "charismatic" and completely open to the Spirit to use their gifts as the Suffering Servant Jesus served His followers. Congar writes on this point:

> In a society such as ours, which is individualistic to the point of anarchy, we must, without losing sight of the extremely profound theme of Christian freedom, remember

the Christian idea of obedience. Obedience is not just a matter of what we have to do for one another, through one another, in view of our common destiny according to the plan of God; obedience effects an important segment of the truth of inter-membral relationships within a differentiated and ordered body (God is not a God of disorder. . . : 1 Co 14:33). While effecting the interlocking of the members in this body, it also effects an acknowledgment of the lordship of Christ, master of order . . . Every Christian encounters Christ in his brothers and in his superiors (even the difficult ones! 1 P 2:118) or subordinates, and he is called to realize his life as a life 'in the Lord,' in this very situation, in these very encounters.[4]

The hierarchical officials receive authority from Christ and are to exercise it according to the mind of Christ, i.e. to the building up of the Church by establishing the best conditions of Church life so that each Christian may be stimulated to live fully according to those gifts which are his.

EACH MEMBER IMPORTANT

If Jesus is present not only in the whole Body but primarily is first present to the individual members, it can be seen why Paul places so much emphasis on the importance of each member living a dynamic Christian life. The life in Christ is a process of growth. Some Christians live as immature children tossed about by every new doctrine (Ep 4:14). They need milk and are not ready for a more solid diet of meat. The sign of their maturity into the "new man" (Ep 2:5; 4:24) is their readiness to put aside their egoism and live for the good of the whole. It is according to the degree of conscious, corporate unity with

Christ, the Head, and all of the members that each individual grows in perfection and can assist in building up the whole body.

Paul puts it very succinctly: "If we live by the truth and in love, we shall grow in all ways into Christ, who is the head . . ." (Ep 4:15). Again he beautifully prays that each member may be given by God the power through His Spirit "for your hidden self to grow strong, so that Christ may live in your hearts through faith, and then, planted in love and built on love . . . knowing the love of Christ which is beyond all knowledge, you are filled with the utter fullness of God" (Ep 3:16-19). The truth that Jesus Christ lives in each of us is shown in the love that we show towards all men. It is love that makes the truth manifest. It is this truth that we have comprehended by the help of the Spirit of the indwelling Jesus that sets us free (Jn 8:32).

All such growth in love of Christ comes from, through and with Him. Yet each member must continue to open up to that presence of Jesus within himself and to Jesus present outside him, in the lives of all men, guiding the whole world into the final completion. Each Christian with St. Paul after Damascus must eagerly seek to find Jesus present as an immanent force, actively working, suffering, rejoicing in His members as His whole Body grows in and through the material created world of God.

Each individual has a unique role to play in reconciling the world, groaning in travail before it is brought to full life. The housewife, teacher, policeman, office-worker, farmer, religious or lay man or woman, all must live consciously in Christ a life of constant response to His lordship as He speaks God's presence in His Word.

A continued purification and conversion away from the dark egoism to the inner light of Jesus within us is needed if we are to live a life of loving service in His Body. Our conversion is a series of saying "yes" to the dictates of Jesus' Spirit. Thus we become "reconcilers." God gave us the work of handing on this reconciliation" (2 Co 5:18). We have the dignity by our service (*diakonia* in Greek) within the Body of Christ to extend the reconciliation by Christ of all things back to His Father.

Jesus is not only the Alpha (Jn 1:2) but He is now, through His members in His Body the Church, inserted into the cosmos and is bringing the material world to its fullness. He is also the Omega, the goal, the end towards which every creature is being drawn as by a magnetic force of personal love.

THE PAROUSIA

The end of the life of Jesus Christ was not to die and enter into His glory solely. Christian doctrine teaches us that Christ will come at the end of time to transform this universe by bringing it to its completion in and through Himself.

> And when everything is subjected to him, then the Son himself will be subject in this turn to the One who subjected all things to him, so that God may be all in all (1 Co 15:28).

Our Christian faith believes therefore that Jesus will complete His work which began after His death and resurrection, continued through His glorious risen life living within His members of His Body, the Church. But in a real sense the *parousia* (Greek word for *presence,* implying the arrival of a person) has already happened since Jesus Christ in His resurrectional life has been present unceasingly. It is not so much another *epiphany,* the coming of Christ from outside into our world as He effected in His incarnation, that we await but the fullness of His diaphany, to use Teilhard de Chardin's term, the "shining through" matter of the living presence of Jesus risen. Jesus is now present and is now effecting the victory over the dark powers of cosmic evil. But in a true sense His victory will be perfect only at the end of time and this is the usual sense in which we use the term *parousia.* It is a gradual transformation through our present history that cannot accept a literal interpretation of the Jewish apocalyptic imagery used in the second epistle of St. Peter:

> The Day of the Lord will come like a thief, and then with a roar, the sky will vanish, the elements will catch fire and fall apart, the earth and all that it contains will be burnt up (2 P 3:10).

The *parousia* will come when the Gospel will have been preached to the entire universe. It is rooted in Christian hope and testifies that Christian redemption includes not merely the spiritual side of mankind, but embraces also the materiality of the whole cosmos. But the Good News is that Jesus Christ is already here bringing about the Kingdom of Heaven in our lives and through us in the whole world. Joseph Bonsirven, a noted New Testament scholar, describes the eschatological message of the Gospels:

> The doctrine of the resurrection of the body on the last day is retained, but there is no description of the Parousia, or of the signs which will precede the Second Coming. Instead, the emphasis is placed on the element of present fulfillment: eternal life is present possession, the spiritual is

already given to us; the Judgment itself is anticipated in the present and so is the Parousia.[5]

CONCLUSION

Jesus Christ is at this moment living within us and is using us, to the degree that we surrender to His leadership, to effect a transformation of the material world into a unified sacrifice of praise and glory to His Heavenly Father. He is not only the Divine Logos, God's exemplar, in whom all things have been created, but He is the same Jesus of Nazareth who evolved under the power of the Holy Spirit to become the full manifestation of God's infinite love for each of us.

By that same Holy Spirit, He broke through sin and death. Darkness had no place any longer as Jesus was raised in glory and given a new relationship to His Father and to us and the whole material world. His Body-Person is now the wonderful presence of the mind of the Father speaking His loving Word to all of us, within us in the depths of our hearts. In an excitingly new way, God now communites Himself to us in our darkness by the bright light of His fully realized Word—Jesus Christ. Into the *dark* silence of our inner world the *brightness* of Jesus enters.

He who was light from all eternity consented to take into His *brightness* the *darkness* of a human consciousness and unconsciousness. He grew into complete resurrectional *brightness* and glory by accepting the *darkness* of temptations, above all, the greatest, to hold on to His life or to lose it out of love for His Father on our behalf. Through obedience He brought His human consciousness and unconscious into an integration.

And now His *brightness* is given to us that we might be led from *darkness* into light. We have seen His glory. But night is approaching. We cry out in hope: "Come, Lord Jesus. Marana tha!" (Rv 22:20).

May you who read this book accept my prayer:

> And we, with our unveiled faces reflecting like mirrors the brightness of the Lord, all grow brighter and brighter as we are turned into the image that we reflect; this is the work of the Lord who is Spirit (2 Co 3:18).

FOOTNOTES

Chapter 1

[1] Cf. S. Bulgakov: "De Verbe Incarné" in: *La Sagesse Divine et la Théanthropie*, (Paris: Aubier, 1943) pp. 65-68.

[2] Cf. G. Maloney, S.J.: *Man-the Divine Icon*, (Pecos, N.M.: Dove, 1973).

[3] E. Brunner: *Man in Revolt*, (London: Lutterworth Press, 1953) pp. 97-98.

[4] St. Irenaeus: *Proof of the Apostolic Preaching;* tr. by J.P. Smith, S.J. in: *Ancient Christian Writers*, (Westminster, Md.: Newman, 1952) vol. 16, ch. 22, p. 61.

[5] I am indebted to P. C. Hodgson: *Jesus-Word and Presence*, (Phil. Pa.: Fortress Press, 1971) p. 118 and to G. Ebeling: *God and Word*, tr. by J. W. Leitch (Phil. Pa.: Fortress Press, 1967 for this idea of God as absolute word.)

[6] M. Allard: "Note sur la formule 'Ehyeh Aser Ehyeh,' " in: *Recherches de Science Religieuse*, 45 no. 1 (Jan-Mar, 1957) pp. 81, 86.

[7] A.J. Heschel: *Man Is Not Alone*, (New York: Harper & Row, 1951) p. 244.

[8] On the *pathos* of God, cf. Robert Wild: *Who I Will be—Is There Joy and Suffering in God?* (Denville, N.J.: Dimension Books, 1976); J. Moltmann: *The Crucified God*, (London: SCM Press, Ltd., 1974) pp. 271-276; A.J. Heschel: *The Prophets*, (N.Y.: Harper & Row, 1971) Vol. II, Ch. 1, "The Theology of Pathos."

[9] J. Moltmann: *The Crucified God*, (London: SCM Press, Ltd., 1974) pp. 272-273.

Chapter 2

[1] Wolfhart Pannenberg: *Jesus—God and Man*, tr. by Lewis L. Wilking & Decane A. Priebe (Philadelphia: The Westminster Press, 1968) p. 33.

[2] Reginald H. Fuller: *The Foundations of New Testament Christology*, (N.Y.: Charles Scribner's Sons, 1965) pp. 232-233, 245-257.

[3] Fuller: *op. cit.*, pp. 173, 197, 243-245.

[4] Paul Evdokimov: *L'Esprit Saint dans la tradition orthodoxe*, (Paris: Ed. du Cerf, 1970) p. 13.

[5] St. Irenaeus: *Adversus Haereses*, Bk. IV, 18, 5; p. 7, 1028-1029.

[6] St. Maximus Confessor: *Quaestiones ad Thalassium*, quaest. 60, *PG* 90, 624A.

[7] Evagrius: *De Oratione*, tr. and ed. by John E. Bamberger, OCSO: *The Praktikos Chapters on Prayer*, (Spencer, Mass: Cistercian Publications, 1970) #60, p. 65.

[8] I am indebted to insights gathered from the writings of Heidegger, Ebeling and Hodgson, especially from the following works: Martin Heidegger: *Being and Time*, tr. by John Macquarrie and Edward Robinson (N.Y.: Harper and Row, 1962); Gerhard Ebeling: *Word and Faith*, tr. by James W. Leitch (Phil.: Fortress Press, 1963); ibid.: *The Nature of Faith*, tr. by R. G. Smith (Phil.: Fortress Press, 1961); P.C. Hodgson: *Jesus— Word and Presence* (Phil.: Fortress Press, 1971).

[9] Otto Procksch: article "Logos" in: *Theological Dictionary of the New Testament*, ed. Gerhard Kittel, ed. and tr. by Geoffrey W. Bromiley, (Grand Rapids: Wm. B. Eerdmans Publishing Co., 1967) p. 92.

[10]G. Kittel: *Theological Dictionary of the New Testament, op. cit.*, pp. 130-132.

[11]Rudolf Bultmann: *Theology of the New Testament*, tr. by Kendrick Grobel, vol. 2 (N.Y.: Charles Scribner's Sons, 1955) p. 62.

[12]Kittel, *op. cit.*, pp. 134-135.

[13]R. Bultmann, *op. cit.*, pp. 60-61; 63.

[14]Elie Wiesel: *Night,* 1969, p. 75.

Chapter 3

[1]For further development on this theme, cf.: J. McKenzie: *The Power and the Wisdom* (Milwaukee: The Bruce Publ. Co., 1965). p. 114ff. Piet Schoonenberg: "He Emptied Himself" Phil. 2, 7, in: *Concilium,* no. 11 (New York: Glen Rock, N.J., 1965) pp. 47-66.

[2]Cf.: Raymond E. Brown, S.J.: *Jesus God and Man,* (Milwaukee: Bruce Publishing Company, 1967); Jacques Guillet, S.J.: *The Consciousness of Jesus,* (New York: Paramus, Toronto: Newman Press, 1972; Piet Schoonenberg, S.J. *The Christ,* (New York: Herder and Herder, 1971).

[3]We repudiate anything that would resemble in any way the 3rd-4th century heresy called, "Patripassianism," that the Father also underwent the passion in the mode of Jesus' body.

[4]Gerald Vann, O.P.: *The Pain of Christ and the Sorrow of God,* (London: Blackfriars, 1947) pp. 67-69.

Chapter 4

[1] A.N. Whitehead: *Process and Reality,* (New York: Macmillan, 1929) pp. 519-520.

[2] Cf. Rudolf Otto: *The Kingdom of God and the Son of Man,* tr. by F. V. Filson and B. Lee-Woolf (Boston: Starr King Press, 1957), pp. 176-218.

[3] Cf. John L. McKenzie: *Dictionary of the Bible,* (Milwaukee: Bruce Publishing Co., 1965) pp. 635-636.

[4] Cf. P. Benoit: "L'Horizon paulinien de l'Epitre aux Ephesiens," in *Exegese et Theologie,* (Paris: Aubier, 1961); *ibid:* "Corps, tête et plerome dans les Epitres de la Captivité," in: *op. cit.* S. Lyonnet, "La redemption de l'univers," in: *Lumiere et Vie,* (Brussels: July-August, 1962); G. Maloney: *The Cosmic Christ from Paul to Teilhard,* (N.Y.: Sheed and Ward, 1968) pp. 17-43.

Chapter 5

[1] J.W. Goethe: *Faust,* tr. by Barker Fairley, (Toronto: University of Toronto Press, 1970) p. 203.

[2] Cf. Ann Belford Ulanov: *The Feminine in Jungian Psychology and in Christian Theology,* (Evanston: Northwestern University Press, 1971) pp. 111 ff. also Karl Stern: *The Flight From Woman,* (N.Y. Farrar, Strauss and Giroux, 1965) pp. 9-73.

[3] C.S. Lewis: *The Abolition of Man,* (N.Y.: Macmillan, 1947).

[4] Dietrich Bonhoeffer: "Thy Kingdom Come" (an essay written in 1932), in: J.D. Godsey: *Preface to Bonhoeffer,* (Philadelphia: Fortress Press, 1965) pp. 28-29.

[5]St. Irenaeus: *Adversus Haereses,* Bk. III, Ch. 19, 1: *The Ante-Nicene Fathers;* Vol. 1; ed. A. Roberts and J. Donaldson, (Grand Rapids: Eerdmans Publishing Co.) pp. 448-449.

[6]G. Fedotov: *A Treasury of Russian Spirituality,* (Gloucester, Mass., Peter Smith, 1969) pp. 216-217.

[7]Nikos Kazantzakis: *The Fratricides,* tr. by A.G. Dallas, (New York: Simon and Schuster, 1964) frontispiece.

Chapter 6

[1]Cf.: the classic work of Ernest Renan: *The Life of Jesus,* (N.Y.: Random House, Modern Library, 1927) and the recent work that brings together all of the rationalists' arguments along with an array of arguments from hypnosis and parapyshology: Preston Harold: *The Shining Stranger; An Unorthodox Interpretation of Jesus and His Mission,* (N.Y.: The Wayfarer Press, 1967). Cf. also: Wm. J. Bryan: *Religious Aspects of Hypnosis,* (Springfield, Ill.: Charles C. Thomas Publisher, 1962), esp. Ch. V: "The Evidence of Jesus Using Hypnosis to Heal," pp. 38ff. For modern psychic healers, cf.: David St. Clair: *Psychic Healers,* (Garden City, N.Y.: Doubleday, 1974).

[2]Cf.: George A. Maloney, S.J.: *Man-the Divine Icon,* (Pecos, N.M.: Dove Publications, 1973) pp. 15ff.

Chapter 7

[1]On the consciousness of Jesus, see: Jacques Guillet, S.J.: *The Consciousness of Jesus;* tr. by Edmond Bonin, (N.Y.: Newman Press, 1972.

[2]Cf.: Yves Congar, O.P.: *Jesus Christ,* tr. by Luke O'Neill, (N.Y.: Herder & Herder, 1966) pp. 66-85.

Chapter 8

[1] G. Maloney: *The Mystic of Fire and Light—St. Symeon, the New Theologian,* (Denville, N.J.: Dimension Bks., 1975) p. 203.

[2] Jurgen Moltmann: *The Crucified God,* (N.Y.: Harper and Row, 1974) pp. 146-147.

[3] Cf.: footnote *q* in *The New Jerusalem Bible,* (N.Y.: Doubleday, 1966) p. 163 as a comment to Jn 7:38. It reads: "From Jesus himself, according to the oldest tradition, though another has joined 'the man who believes in me' with what follows, making the 'streams' flow from the believer."

[4] On this point, see the excellent presentation by Hugo Rahner, S.J.: "The Beginnings of the Devotion in Patristic Times," in: *Heart of the Savior,* ed. by Josef Stierli, (N.Y.: Herder & Herder, 1957) pp. 37-57.

[5] Cited by H. Rahner, *op. cit.,* p. 54.

Chapter 9

[1] On this point cf.: F.X. Durrwell, C.SS.R.: *The Resurrection,* tr. by Rosemary Sheed (N.Y.: Sheed & Ward, 1966) pp. 1-34.

[2] Jurgen Moltmann: *Theology of Hope,* (N.Y.: Harper & Row, 1967) pp. 76-84, 172-182, 302.

[3] *Ibid.,* p. 181.

[4] Durrwell, *op. cit.,* p. 8.

[5] Cf.: Hogdson, *op. cit.,* pp. 220-291.

[6] Durrwell, *op. cit.,* pp. 130-132.

[7]*Ibid.*, pp. 108 ff.

[8]Cf.: footnote *1* in: *The Jerusalem Bible*, p. 341.

[9]Cf.: G. Maloney, S.J.: *The Cosmic Christ from Paul to Teilhard*, (N.Y.: Sheed & Ward, 1968) chs. 1 & 2.

[10]For the fuller meaning of the term: *anakephaloioomai* cf.: H. Schlier, Anakephaloioomai, in: *Theologisches Worterbuch*, Vol. III (Stuttgart: W. Kohlhammer, 1938) pp. 681 ff.

[11]Joseph Huby: *Les Epitres dè la Captivité*, (Paris: Beauchesne, 1935) p. 40, cited by Christopher Mooney, S.J.: "The Body of Christ in the Writings of Teilhard de Chardin," in: *Theological Studies*, 25 (Dec., 1964) pp. 604-605.

Chapter 10

[1]I recommend on this topic: Flloyd V. Filson: *Jesus Christ: The Risen Lord*, (Nashville: Abingdon Press, 1956).

Chapter 11

[1]F.X. Durrwell: *op. cit.*, p. 210.

[2]Pierre Benoit: "Corps, tête, et plerome dan les Epitres de la Captivite," in: *Exegese et Theologie*, (Paris: Aubier, 1961) p. 147.

[3]Yves Congar, O.P., *Jesus Christ*, tr. by Luke O'Neill, (N.Y.: Herder & Herder, 1966) pp. 131-143.

[4]Yves Congar, *op. cit.*, pp. 193-194.

[5]Joseph Bonsirven, S.J.: *Theology of the New Testament*, (Westminster, Md.: Newman Press, 1962) p. 148.